Inclusive Education of Learners with Disability – The Theory versus Reality

STUDIES IN PHILOSOPHY, CULTURE
AND CONTEMPORARY SOCIETY

Edited by Bogusław Paź

VOLUME 30

PETER LANG

Zenon Gajdzica/ Robin McWilliam/ Miloň Potměšil/ Guo Ling

Inclusive Education of Learners with Disability – The Theory versus Reality

PETER LANG

Bibliographic Information published by the Deutsche Nationalbibliothek
The Deutsche Nationalbibliothek lists this publication in the Deutsche
Nationalbibliografie; detailed bibliographic data is available online at
http://dnb.d-nb.de.

Library of Congress Cataloging-in-Publication Data
A CIP catalog record for this book has been applied for at the
Library of Congress.

This publication was financially supported by University of Silesia in Katowice, Poland.

UNIVERSITY OF SILESIA
IN KATOWICE

Czech Republic: The chapter was supported by grants: TL03000679 CZ
and US-WEINOE 1S-1213-001-1-10-06.

China: The chapter was supported by grant: Leshan Normal University
Co-building project: SC16XK082.

Reviewer: Prof. Stanisława Byra, UMCS.

ISSN 2196-0151 · ISBN 978-3-631-83418-3 (Print)
E-ISBN 978-3-631-84021-4 (E-PDF) · E-ISBN 978-3-631-84022-1 (EPUB)
E-ISBN 978-3-631-84023-8 (MOBI) · DOI 10.3726/b17782

CONTENTS

Preface 11

Chapter 1 Inclusive education of learners with disability in
Polish experiences..13

1.1. Theoretical foundations of inclusive education 13

1.1.1. Historical outline of education for learners
with disability in Poland 13

1.1.2. Polish concepts of inclusive education 17

1.1.3. Cultural determinants of inclusive
education 26

1.2. Inclusive education in practice 29

1.2.1. Organization of inclusive education 29

1.2.2. Financing the education of learners with
disabilities 36

1.2.3. Competences and qualifications of teachers
in inclusive education 38

1.2.4. Principles of work in the inclusive class 43

1.2.5. Barriers to the development of inclusive
education 50

1.2.6. Developmental prospects of inclusive
education 52

Conclusion 55

References 57

Chapter 2 Inclusive education of learners with disability in the
United States of America 67

Introduction 67

Competing Values 67

American societal values of self-determination and
independence 68

American cultural values of equity and fairness 70

    Reject monarchy 70

    Home for religious tolerance 70

    ADA and IDEA 70

2.1. Theoretical foundations of inclusive education 71

    2.1.1. Historical outline of education for disabled
    learners in the USA 71

        The early history 71

        Building support for inclusion 72

        Reservations about inclusion 73

        Research related to inclusion and program
        effectiveness 73

        Teacher attitudes towards inclusion 73

        The adolescence of inclusive practices 74

        Curriculum-based measurement 75

        Classroom instruction in inclusive settings 75

        Inclusion in secondary schools 76

        Inclusive education and students with severe
        disabilities 76

    2.1.2. Major approaches to inclusive education 77

    2.1.3. Cultural determinants of inclusive education 79

2.2. Inclusive education in practice 81

    2.2.1. Organization of inclusive education 81

    2.2.2. Financing inclusive education 84

    2.2.3. Competencies and qualifications of inclusive
    education teachers 86

    2.2.4. What happens in an inclusive class 86

    2.2.5. Barriers to the development of inclusive
    education 88

    2.2.6. The future of inclusive education 89

Conclusion 89

References 90

Chapter 3 Inclusive education in the Czech Republic 97

    3.1 Theoretical foundations of inclusive education 97

    Terminology 97

    Historical background of education for the
disabled in the Czech National Conception 101

    3.2. Inclusive education in practice in the Czech
Republic (2018) 104

    The educational system in the Czech Republic 104

    State education in the Czech Republic 105

    Pre-primary education 105

    Primary school 105

    Secondary schools 105

    Tertiary education 106

    Inclusive education 106

    Supportive measures – level I 108

    Supportive measures – levels II–V 108

    School advisory facilities and their role in
inclusive education 109

    Education of talented learners 109

    Individual educational plan 110

    The current quantification indicators of
education in the Czech Republic 110

    Primary education 114

    Secondary education 116

    Disabled learners from the perspective of
classmates without disability 122

    Introduction 122

    Attitudes and adolescents 123

    Characterization of the target group 124

    Methodology of data collection and processing ... 126

    Research sample and its characterization 126

    Conclusions 129

    Recommendations for school practice 130

Sentiments, attitudes and concerns of teaching staff
in regard to inclusive education 131

  Introduction 131

    Methodology of data collection and processing ... 132

    The research sample and its composition 133

    Analysis and processing of research data 133

    Age of respondents 134

Education of respondents 134

Respondents' occupation 134

Contact with disabled people 135

The perception of respondents' professional
readiness 135

Awareness of the legislative background concerning
the upbringing and education of disabled learners 136

Confidence in educating disabled learners 136

Perception of experience with education of disabled
learners 137

Awareness of the opportunities to get professional
help 137

Statistical analysis of the collected data 137

Factor Analysis 137

Correlation of scales with variables 138

Sources influencing participants' opinions, concerns
and attitudes 138

Conclusion 141

  Factor Analysis 141

  Inclusive education in the Czech Republic:
  conclusions 142

References 144

Chapter 4 Inclusive education of learners with disability in China ... 147

  Introduction 147

4.1. Theoretical foundations of inclusive education 148

4.1.1. Historical outline of education for disabled
learners in China 148

Historical background of education for
learners with disabilities 148

Corresponding stages of education for
learners with disabilities 150

The preparation phase: the sprout of
ancient thought about special education 150

The formation phase: the emergence of
modern special education schools 151

The vigorous growth phase: the
establishment of modern special education
system 152

4.1.2. Concepts of inclusive education in China 155

Understanding of inclusive education in
China 156

Understanding of inclusion 157

Understanding of inclusive education 158

Relations between inclusive education,
special education and general education 160

4.1.3. Learning in Regular Class (LRC) – the
Chinese form of inclusive education 161

4.1.4. Cultural determinants of LRC 163

Moral ideas of Confucianism 164

Value orientations of pragmatism 165

4.2. Inclusive education in practice 167

4.2.1. Development of LRC 167

4.2.2. Organization of LRC 170

4.2.3. Eligibility for LRC 171

4.2.4. Admission to LRC 171

4.2.5. Management of LRC 172

The responsibilities of general school in the
practice of LRC 173

The responsibilities of special education
resource centre in the practice of LRC 174

The responsibilities of special education
school in the practice of LRC 175

4.2.6. Combined regular and special curriculum
for LRC learners 175

4.2.7. Financial mechanisms of LRC 178

Financial input for special education 178

Financial input for LRC 180

4.2.8. Competences and qualifications of
inclusive education teachers 182

Qualification for LRC teachers 183

Qualification for resource room teachers 184

Qualification for itinerant teachers 185

4.2.9. Barriers to the development of inclusive
education 186

Exam-oriented value of education in
China 186

Contradictory attitudes to inclusive
education 187

Imperfect policy and regulations from
government 188

Lack of funding guarantee 189

Shortage of qualified LRC teachers 190

4.2.10. Developmental prospects of inclusive
education 191

Conclusion 192

References 193

Name Index 199

Preface

The notion of inclusive education is applied to educational processes with ambiguity, vagueness, and controversy. As a consequence, it is often used in various connotations which provide it with the meaning of: a scientific theory, a concept of educational transformations, an ideology, a model of education, a methodological concept, organizational work, a set of educational conditions, occurring processes or even of a paradigm. In scientific debates, inclusion is located near educational integration; as regards its contents – it is associated with equality, acceptance, and normalization; it is opposed to: exclusion, marginalization, rejection, depreciation. The diversified approach to inclusion in the theory of social sciences is determined by many factors. Among them, the major ones are sociocultural determinants and those associated with the development of educational sciences. Therefore, it should not be surprising that the process of developing social and educational inclusion differs significantly in many countries. This results in a variety of diverse practices aimed at the development of inclusive culture at school and in the environments which surround it. What might serve as a simple example is the influence of the multicultural environment on the development and the essence of the way in which inclusion is understood. In multicultural environments, it is a natural result of culturally diversified experiences of learners, their parents and teachers – their attitude to traditions, customs, beliefs. They constitute a specific habitus of the recognized values, norms, aspirations, and attitudes towards the surrounding reality. In these environments, the functional limitation resulting from disability is one of many differentiating factors and disability itself is more frequently treated as a product of social interactions. Due to this, teachers and learners can be more easily convinced to view disability in a relative way. In the environments with smaller cultural diversity, disability is a more distinctly differentiating property. In such environments, the culture of inclusion must take a longer route and make bigger effort to overcome the focus on disability in the medical and functional dimension.

What has due significance are historical experiences of the whole nations (such as Holocaust or apartheid) and the concept of education for
the humanistic values of equality, respect for unlikeness, justice, which has
been built to a smaller or larger extent on these experiences. The culture
of inclusion is also largely influenced by political processes. In politics, the
domination of extreme right-wing views, which glorify the significance of
race and origin and induce fear of otherness, does not enhance educational
inclusion.

The diversified perception and advancement of inclusion has its sources
also in the development of educational science, particularly special education. The deeply rooted practices of separated school undermine the development of inclusive culture. As a result, school inclusion is often treated as
a development and evolution of special education – as its reconstruction.
However, in the cultures with weaker traditions of separated education, it
is easier to shape inclusive environments based on the deconstruction of
special education.

These are just a few selected examples which illustrate what different
ways inclusion has to take in particular cultures and countries. This book
is aimed at presenting these determinants and the resulting practices of
inclusive education in four countries which, in many respects, differ from
each other: Poland, the United States, the Czech Republic, and China.

Zenon Gajdzica

Chapter I Inclusive education of learners with disability in Polish experiences

1.1. Theoretical foundations of inclusive education

1.1.1. Historical outline of education for learners with disability in Poland

The development of special education for learners with disability in Poland has taken place in a way typical of Central European countries. It has been related to social, cultural and economic changes. However, certain specificity of Polish educational transformations should be emphasized here as well. Among other things, the changes have been associated with: the specific hermetization determined by a long period of Poland's functioning within the socialist block, strong influences of the Church on social life and still relatively unchanging monoculturalism, which plays a significant role not only in shaping the attitudes to the Other but also in creating the culture of inclusive education.

The interrelation between educational transformations and sociocultural changes is undisputable. This dependence can be also seen in the transformations in the basic assumptions of both education of the disabled and the conceptualization of the system of special education. With certain generalization, four basic fields of transformations affecting the shape of education for the disabled can be indicated:

- evolution of social attitudes towards people with disability;
- legal changes;
- development of institutions aimed at care, education and rehabilitation of the disabled;
- scientific advancement (especially of special education, psychology, medicine, sociology, social anthropology) which determines the change of views on the essence of disability.

Each of these factors has been of crucial significance in transforming and revaluing the views on the educational needs of the discussed group of learners.

What can become a starting point for a short description of these factors is the changing social attitude to the disabled. It is this change which has determined other transformations in the field of law and school education. The changes in social attitudes to the disabled have not basically differed from the changes taking place in other European countries. The Middle Ages were known for the use of rigorous educational methods. Literature provides many descriptions concerning cruel treatment of people with disturbed development to the point of regarding them as social burden. The opinions promoting the need of care for the disabled started in the 14th century. This can be confirmed by the Wiślica Statute of 1347, in which disabled people were defended. Slightly later, the first attempts at taking care for the disabled were made. This was usually done in the form of alms-houses run by monks. In the 17th century, the first care houses appeared, sometimes also conducted by landowners and farmers' groups. Until the mid-19th century, the needs of disabled people were identified only with care. Since that period, the needs pertaining to education have been focused on as well (Balcerek, 1981; Doroszewska, 1989; Wyczesany, 2005; Gajdzica, Franiok, 2013).

Alongside the popularization of elementary education, the problem of disabled children became more visible. They could not manage in the widely accessible form of education. Therefore, special schools for them were organized. The first such school for learners with mild intellectual disability was founded in Poznań in 1896. In the early 20th century, such institutions were established in many big towns. After the Second World War, the number of special schools substantially increased. This was also a result of the intensive development of theoretical and methodological foundations of work with this group of learners. The tasks in this field were fulfilled by the workers of the National Institute of Special Pedagogy, founded by Maria Grzegorzewska in Warsaw in 1922 (Pilecka, Pilecki, 2002). The First Polish Congress of Special Education Teachers took place in 1925 and the act on the system of education in Poland was issued in 1932. It comprised the statement that education of "not normal" children should be conducted in institutions, mainstream schools, special schools and special classes. Before the Second World War, there were only primary schools for disabled children in Poland. In fact, there were neither vocational schools preparing for work nor institutions for children with more profound disability. Thus, after the Second World War, special school education developed on the basis of primary school. In the 1950s, the number of special primary schools tripled and vocational education developed simultaneously. In subsequent years, "schools of life" started to be founded for learners with moderate and profound intellectual disability (earlier they did not attend schools at all) as well as special kindergartens. Since 1994, school obligation has comprised children with profound mental disability. Nowadays, they most frequently attend classes conducted in educational-therapeutic groups (Dziedzic, 1977; Balcerek, 1981; Wyczesany, 2005; Gajdzica, Franiok, 2013).

The social transformations initiated in Poland at the turn of the 1980s and 1990s drew more attention to integrating tendencies. In the Polish tradition (both in science and practical activities), integrated education is distinctly differentiated from inclusive education. The concept of integrated education introduced into the Polish system of education has been borrowed from Germany, where it is sometimes referred to as the Hamburg model. Its characteristic features are: two teachers in a class (early education/subject teacher and special education teacher), 3–5 learners with disability in a class, not more than 20 learners in a class, implementation of all lessons in the common, shared space.

In the early 1990s, integrated education comprised a statistically small group of disabled learners. Currently, the significance of this form of education has largely increased in Poland. However, learners with profound or multiple disability still mostly attend special schools (Apanel, 2016).

A few new forms of care for the disabled appeared in the early 1990s – rehabilitation-educational (care) centres, family communities, and occupational therapy workshops. Some of them are run by various foundations and associations for the disabled (Wyczesany, 2005). The early 2000s was a period focused on inclusive tendencies, based on conscious organization of including learners with disabilities into mainstream schools. It seems worth highlighting that hidden inclusion has been present in the Polish system of education for many years (Hulek, 1992). Yet, it has resulted from an imperfect system of legal certification, the lack of special schools in disabled learners' regions and the ignoring of special educational needs of these learners.

While making an overview of the transformations in the educational system for learners with disability in recent decades, three periods can be distinguished as regards the legal acts regulating the organization of the school system:

- the first period: before introducing the formal legal determinants of integrated education in 1991;[1]
- the second period: the years of the so called prime of integrated education, between 1991–2010;
- the third period: after the acceptance in the 2010 of a package of directives,[2] describing the entire changes in education of learners with special educational needs, the organization and provision of

---

1   The Act on the educational system of 7th September 1991 (Journal of Laws, No 67 of 1996, p. 329 with changes) ensured the possibility of this educational form in all types of schools, in compliance with individual developmental and educational needs of children and youth. The Directive No 29 of the Minister of National Education of 4th October 1993 on the principles of organizing care for disabled learners, their education in mainstream and integrated public kindergartens, schools, centres, and on the organization of special education (Official Journal of the Ministry of National Education of 15th November 1993) provided the detailed conditions for the organization of integrated classes and groups as well as integrated schools and kindergartens.

2   These are the directives of the Ministry of National Education accepted on 17th November 2010 (Journal of Laws, No 228):
    1) on providing and organizing psychological-pedagogical aid in public kindergartens, schools and centres,
    2) on the conditions for organizing the education and care for disabled and socially maladjusted children and youth in mainstream or integrated kindergartens, schools and classes,
    3) on the conditions for organizing the education and care for disabled and socially maladjusted children and youth in special kindergartens, schools, classes and centres,
    4) changing the previous directive on the conditions, the way of assessing, grading and promoting learners and on conducting tests and examinations in public,
    5) on the detailed principles of the activity of public psychological-pedagogical counselling centres, including public specialist centres,

psychological-pedagogical support – the period of more intensive activities for the development of inclusive education (Cytowska, 2016, p. 190).

Summarizing this, it should be stated that:

- social changes have enhanced educational transformations. Slightly simplifying, they have evolved from rejecting and ignoring the needs of the disabled, through accepting their right to care and later to segregated education, to the recognition of their right to integration and full autonomy;
- legal transformations at first enabled but later necessitated the obligatory education of disabled children and youth, they have been favourable for creating "flexible" educational pathways, tailored to the needs and potentialities of a child;
- the increasing knowledge concerning the mechanisms of the development and the learning process of the disabled has facilitated the development of various forms of fulfilling educational needs of disabled learners (Gajdzica, Franiok, 2013).

1.1.2. Polish concepts of inclusive education

The attempts at constructing the theoretical foundations of inclusive education have developed in three currents. The first two are associated mostly with education of disabled learners, the third – with other disfavoured groups (e.g. national minorities, immigrant children, learners from poor environments).

The first current is typical of pedagogy concerning the disabled in the countries of Central Europe. It is based on the evolution (reconstruction) of the assumptions of special education and on adjusting them to the needs of inclusive education.

The second current, to a large extent borrowed from practical experiences and scientific research of West Europe, Scandinavia and North America, is grounded in the idea of deconstruction of special education

---

6) on the status of public psychological-pedagogical counselling centres, including public specialist centres.

and creating, on the basis of its negative experiences, the assumptions of the culture of inclusive school (Thomas, Loxley, 2007). The current is associated with the premise that inclusive education is not a new version of special education. It is assumed that such treatment of inclusive education would limit its potentialities or even destroy its innovativeness. Thus, broadly understood inclusive education ought to be treated as a subdiscipline of pedagogy, not a new version of special education (Hinz, 2009, p. 172; qtd. after Szumski, 2010, p. 41).

The third current refers to the notion of inclusion to the smallest extent. However, it is compliant with its assumed diversity and the motto of school for everyone. This current makes use mostly of the experiences and the theory of multi- and intercultural education. In its assumptions, it most frequently refers (apart from the obvious relations to sociology and intercultural psychology) to social pedagogy (Lewowicki, Ogrodzka-Mazur, Szczurek-Boruta, 2000; Szkudlarek, 2003; Lewowicki, 2011).

Despite many significant differences between these concepts, especially as regards their origins, they have the common core – the diversity of a group and the creation of conditions for possibly the fullest development of all learners. In practice, with growing frequency – all the three currents overlap in many fields – often without (I would risk this statement) the awareness of the authors of the studies presenting their basic assumptions. Therefore, in the Polish expert literature, it is more and more difficult to find descriptions of the concept of inclusion which present a pure form located entirely in one current. This results from:

• the diffusion of scientific disciplines and subdisciplines due to the tendency towards interdisciplinary treating of the discourse within educational sciences. This brings about the migration of notions, concepts and ideas not only among educational subdisciplines but also among scientific disciplines. What may serve as an example is the collaboration of special and social educationalists, among other things, in the field of the conceptualization of social inclusion;
• the use in Polish scientific works and in practical activities of the concepts (solutions, experiences) elaborated and described in the countries of West Europe and North America. What might become a well-aimed example here as well are the concepts of educational inclusion.

In the further part, the characteristics of the first current of educational inclusion will be focused on. It is the most visible one in Polish scientific research. In its certain variety, it constitutes the basic set of information used in creating social practices of educating learners with disability. It should be emphasized here that this concept is neither mature nor original because the Polish scientific literature is not rich in works which, strictly speaking, compose the theoretical foundations of the discussed form of education. In the descriptions of these foundations, the authors often refer to works in English, also to the experiences of Scandinavian and Central European countries. The characterization will start with an introduction of the notion of inclusion and its location in the system of categories applied in pedagogy.

In spite of its growing popularity in scientific works, the term "inclusion" is ignored in Polish pedagogical dictionaries and lexicons (even those on special and intercultural education) (see: Milerski, Śliwerski, 2000; Okoń, 2004; Kupisiewicz, Kupisiewicz, 2009; Guzik-Tkacz, Siegień-Matyjewicz, 2015). The analysis of literature in the field of pedagogy and related sciences shows that the notion of (social, educational) inclusion is often used in various connotations which give it the sense of: a scientific theory, a concept of educational changes, an ideology, a model of education, a concept of methodological or organizational work, a set of educational conditions, some occurring processes, a paradigm (Zamkowska, 2009; Szumski, 2010; Kruk-Lasocka, 2012; Ligus, 2012; Gajdzica, Bełza, 2016). In scientific debates, educational inclusion is frequently situated near educational integration and, in terms of contents, it is associated with: equality, acceptance, and normalization; and is opposed to: exclusion, marginalization, rejection, and depreciation (Szumski, 2010; Firkowska-Mankiewicz, 2012; Olszewski, Parys, 2016; Gajdzica, Bełza, 2016).

The Polish experience of several decades of strong Soviet influences in pedagogy enhanced isolation. In the field of theory and practice, this hindered the permeating of innovative views on education of learners with disabilities. These hindrances can be spotted in several areas:

• The first is associated with the domination of the positivist paradigm in practicing educational sciences. The scientistic approach has resulted in locating the issues of education mostly in functional and structural currents.

- The second area has been determined by the domination of the medical model of disability. For many years, it was treated as a determinant of viewing the potentialities and limitations of learners with disability. This brought about some consequences in glorifying the nosological diagnosis and in viewing a disabled learner through therapeutic processes.
- The third area comprises the problems of creating the educational system for disabled learners limited to special school education based on segregation and separation.
- The fourth is strictly compliant with the policy of success, which made the censorship-free discourse on education impossible. This impeded the detection and indication of mistakes, of the ambiguity and disastrous effects of reformatory decisions both in the field of science or higher education (preparing future teachers) and in practical solutions.

Obviously, the indicated fields of creating the theory of education for the discussed group of learners have come into being not only on the basis of the aforementioned isolation of Poland but also as a result of certain economic, cultural and social conditions. It should be stressed that these currents and the related practical solutions were also present in the countries with much longer democratic traditions. What seems worth mentioning is that the political situation in Poland until 1989 has substantially consolidated the existing state and delayed the transformations leading to the pluralistic model of practicing science and the creation of diverse educational practices. The period after 1989, however, was full of attempts to make up for the lost time. This was often based on applying some borrowed models. These processes did not involve deeper reflection upon errors of equivalence, associated with a different economic and cultural situation of Poland.

On the foundations of the reborn democracy, more significance was attributed to the aspirations to much fuller social participation of the disabled. This was favourable for recognizing the right to choosing the form of education for disabled learners also in mainstream schools. It is worth emphasizing that that time was a period of still insufficient willingness towards full inclusion. Therefore, an attempt was made to adopt the Hamburg model of institutional integration in the Polish environment.

The discussion on the strong and weak points of this model will be omitted here as they have been described in many works (e.g. Zamkowska, 2000; Bąbka, 2001; Szumski, 2006; Gajdzica, 2011; Gajdzica, 2013; Apanel, 2016). Yet, what is worth highlighting is the qualitative change in education, brought about by integrated teaching. In the 1990s, it was an attempt at going beyond the regimen of segregating and separating fulfilment of school duty for learners with disability.

The popularization of integrated kindergarten and school groups intensified the discussion on the integrated form of education. Most frequently, it had been confronted so far with education in special centres. The transformations resulted in the development of the discourse and the need for research into different educational forms. A multitude of scientific works dealing with various aspects of integrated education (e.g. socialization in a group, conflicts, stereotypes, prejudice, collaboration, rivalry, methods of work, acquisition of skills) has resulted in many attempts at elaborating the theoretical foundations of integrated education. These foundations, based on studies, have revealed many negative consequences of institutional integration, deeply rooted in the concept itself and in defective forms of its implementation (e.g. Bąbka, 2001; Szumski, 2006; Gajdzica, 2011). Not without some risk, it can be stated that – alongside the paradigmatic diversification in pedagogy, the rising social awareness and the consolidation of democracy – the criticism of institutional integration has become the basis for the conceptualization of educational inclusion and its practical advancement. This is illustrated in the tables which shows the differences between particular types of education for learners with disability (Table 1).

In practice, it is difficult to mark an unambiguous caesura indicating the breakthrough towards educational inclusion in Poland. This moment can be probably marked and viewed in several perspectives on the basis of diversified criteria. In the aspect of inclusive education (treating it, in compliance with the applied concept, as the continuation of separated and integrated education), the following perspectives seem most important: the scientific, sociocultural, political standpoint as well as the perspective of educational practice.

Table 1. Differences between the segregated, integrated and inclusive approach (source: Firkowska-Mankiewicz, 2012)

Segregated approach	Integrated approach	Inclusive approach
Education for some	Education for almost all	Education for all
Focus on the subject and curriculum	Focus on the learner	Focus on the class
The same curriculum for all learners	Individual curriculum for disabled children	The teaching strategy for teachers
Emphasis on teaching	Emphasis on teaching and learning	Emphasis on learning and solving problems together
Diagnostic approach focusing on deficiencies	Approach aimed at seeking the learner's weak and strong points	Holistic approach focusing on potentialities
Placing the learner in a segregated school	Placing the learner in an appropriate programme	Adjusting the conditions of the regular school class
The teacher who is helpless without a specialist	The teacher collaborating with a specialist	The teacher becomes a specialist and takes responsibility for all children – with and without disability

In Polish scientific studies, the classical transformation of topoi (kept in collective thinking about particular cultural patterns which constitute both arguments in discussion and reference points for the considered phenomena, processes, states, etc.) concerning the place and the basic assumptions of education for disabled learners has been related to several changes. In most general terms, they pertain to the migration of notions (Koselleck, 2009; 2012) and cross-paradigmatic moves (Krause, 2004; 2010). What seems of key significance in this process is the migration of the notion of disability.

The starting point for the transformations analysed in this way is the assumption that notions have their own history and that, despite their unchanged linguistic contents, migration takes place within their meanings (Koselleck, 2009, pp. 59–61). The example of such a notion (of key rank for the discussed change of topoi) is *disability*. The changes of its sense have been associated not only with historical transformations but also with the interdisciplinary moving across sciences. This is mostly related to liberating the contents of the notion from interdependence within disciplines, which completes but also burdens these contents with the findings typical of a particular discipline. The interdisciplinary migration of the notion of disability brings about attributing different meanings to it in particular contexts. Disability applies the problem arranged form only when it is confronted with the subjects burdened with it and their environment. Providing disability with the dimension of property, feature, state and phenomenon, as well as taking into account its dynamics and processuality as the basis of a scientific problem, necessitate transgressing the borders of disciplinary knowledge and encourage to apply a multi-paradigmatic research approach (Gajdzica, 2017, pp. 212–213). At first, the notion of disability was viewed mainly through disorders of the organism (dysfunctions of its particular organs) and individual functionality, rooted in the behavioural and cognitive concepts of humanity. This is reflected not only in the changes in perceiving a person with disability but also in the advancement in particular types of rehabilitation, in noticing and eliminating barriers, in the organization of social support in the consecutive historical periods (Garbat, 2015). The changes in special education and in other social disciplines have moved researchers' interest not so much towards what have caused disability but rather towards what causes it. This has attributed the dynamic dimension to disability. It is worth recalling that Reinhart Koselleck is of the opinion that attributing dynamics to historical notions is a typical symptom of their migration (Koselleck, 2012). This turn was associated with placing disability in the field of social interactions and with noticing its relative nature, depending on diverse points of reference. As a result, disability has become a scientific problem – not only medical and psychological but also sociocultural one. This transition is reflected in cross-paradigmatic clashes within special education (Krause, 2010) and other disciplines – the clashes which create various (identical, parallel, contradictory) worlds of disabled people (Gajdzica, 2017, p. 213).

The transformations in the perception of learners with disability and their educational needs are based on analogous foundations. Their starting point was also the criticism of individual (medical and later functional) models and the recognition of social models as the leading ones. These transformations were compliant with the changes of the leading paradigms and they determined these changes as well. They can be treated as the transition from the positivistic paradigm (built on biologism and rehabilitation processes) to the humanistic paradigm (based on social and environmental premises of the functioning of disabled people, on the normalization processes concerning the environment of their life and on emancipation) (Krause, 2010). These changes were identical with the transformations in West Europe and North America (e.g. Rieser, 2013; Speck, 2013).

As stated earlier, it is difficult to indicate the accurate caesura of the scientific breakthrough in Poland, which consisted in a paradigmatic transition, a change of the dominating model of disability and in thinking about the education for disabled learners aimed at inclusion. It seems that the turn took place in the 1990s – later than in Scandinavia and West Europe. As it usually happens, it was associated with the publication of some significant studies. However, they did not have impact on the discussed changes immediately. As regards inclusion of the disabled, in my opinion these were the following works: *Oblicza upośledzenia [Faces of Disability]* by Małgorzata Kościelska (1995), *Integracyjne złudzenie ponowoczesności [The integrative illusion of post-modernity]* by Amadeusz Krause (2000) and the texts in the collective work entitled *Upośledzenie w społecznym zwierciadle [Disability in the social mirror]* (Gustavsson, Zakrzewska-Manterys, 1997), as well as scientific, methodological and publicistic studies in some collective works edited by Jadwiga Bogucka and Małgorzata Kościelska (e.g. 1994; 1996).

The discussed breakthrough was also largely influenced by free access to foreign literature and the first translations into Polish of some works published in the countries with longer traditions of non-segregated education (e.g. Fairbairn, Fairbairn, 2000). Slightly later (in the late 2000s), some works appeared entirely dedicated to theoretical foundations of inclusive education (Zacharuk, 2008) and to the presentation of some broader studies on this form of education, grounded in the reliable theoretical base (Szumski, 2010). Especially the second work can be recognized as a turning point in creating the theoretical foundations of inclusion in Poland.

The revival of humanistic pedagogy and paradigmatic changes in special education has enhanced the reflection upon the perception and definition of a learner with special needs. In general, four concepts associated with particular pedagogical currents can be distinguished:

- based on the medical aspect, determined by the notion of physiological norm, focusing on damages of the organism. Its main idea is dynamizing the learner's development. For many years, this approach prevailed in the thinking about disabled learners within educational sciences;
- viewed in the context of special educational needs. It results from the belief in dissimilarity of needs due to dysfunctions in fulfilling functional norms. This is particularly visible in psychological concepts;
- based on the association with special fulfilment of common needs. Within this standpoint, learners' needs are not differentiated (convergence of the needs of all learners is assumed) and the focus is on providing special support for learners with difficulties in implementing the common core curriculum in order to include them into mainstream education;
- defined from the constructivist perspective. This concept assumes building an image of the disabled learner in the course of interactions within the class. It is important here to create some mechanisms based on relations and to outline the areas of educational norm and the currents of common educational influences. Educational activities are aimed at inclusion through normalization of the school situation with the assumption of variety as the starting point for all educational activities (Gajdzica 2010, p. 163).

These concepts can be matched with particular forms of educating learners with disabilities. The first is compliant with the traditional separating approach – education in special centres, especially in the years preceding the (earlier discussed) paradigmatic turn. The second concept, typical of the initial period of institutional integration in Poland, was predominant in education in the 1990s. The third is associated with the model of inclusion implemented as the continuation of special education but with regard to the modification of basic assumptions of special education as the foundation for inclusion. The fourth concept is written into the assumptions of inclusive education, earlier specified as deconstruction of special education, which breaks with its assumptions and is located in general pedagogy.

Summing up, the concept of educational inclusion in the Polish conditions has the following characteristics:

- referring to the humanistic foundations of pedagogy and its multi-paradigmatic character;
- drawing knowledge and experience from the output of special education;
- treating the processes of inclusion as a form of special education located in mainstream schools;
- viewing the organization of inclusive processes as the continuation and a more humanistic form of separated and integrated education;
- emphasizing the social model of disability;
- emphasizing the categories of the mainstream and special educational needs;
- viewing support as an important element of inclusive processes;
- incidental referring to the organizational culture of school as the basis of the processes of inclusion.

1.1.3. Cultural determinants of inclusive education

Each school develops a microclimate influenced by social relations, attitudes, norms and rules which shape them – it is a derivative of some external and internal factors. The culture of school, as an element of the broadly understood culture, comprises the beliefs, views, attitudes, relations and principles which shape all the aspects in which school functions as an institution, organization and community (Czerepaniak-Walczak, 2015, p. 80). Obviously, the basis for its maintenance and co-creation is the knowledge of these components.

To a certain extent, the culture of school reflects the culture which surrounds it. Yet, this does not mean that it must be totally analogous to its local or glocal varieties. It is particularly visible while analysing the dominating functions of a particular school. If it is assumed that the main goal of school is the transmission of culture (shaping a learner to the conformist life and to the perpetuation of the existing order), the culture of school should enhance this by being compliant with the surrounding culture. However, if the aim is preparing a learner for active and emancipated activity and co-creation of culture, the culture of school should at least partially go beyond the framework of local culture. In this approach, school education can and should precede the development of inclusive social culture and should indicate its prospects. They can refer to three fields:

- the first – which comprises the shaping of respect for the values which constitute the foundations of inclusion;
- the second – the elimination of the barriers, especially the mental ones based on the culture of ability and the rejection of unlikeness;
- the third – consisting in preparing learners for acting for inclusive culture.

This preparation has two components: the motivational (encouraging to authentic acting for people in a worse life situation) and the cognitive one (equipping with the knowledge of the needs and ways of rational reacting to learners' unlikeness).

Among other things, this is the reason why the inclusive culture of school can come into being only on the basis of the inclusive culture of the environment. The latter is strictly associated with the attitudes towards people with disability (in a broader sense, also Others – unique in a visible way), with the recognition of their values and the benefits of acting for them and for the whole local and glocal community. The attitudes to Others/Aliens are shaped in many ways. Still, it is the knowledge of them and the direct contact with them which constitutes their common foundation.

Poland is a country of relatively low cultural and religious diversity. The historical sources of this situation may be sought in the migration of minorities to the foreign land in the post-war period, the isolation of the country and the unification policy conducted by the communist authorities. Therefore – since the early 1990s, the relations of Poles with immigrants and cultural (also religious and denominational) minorities have been less frequent than of the inhabitants of the countries on the other side of the iron curtain. The residents of borderlands are an exception, as they have experienced the multiculturalism of borderlands in a natural way. This situation has also influenced the attitudes towards disabled people, who are often viewed as other or even alien. To a certain extent, they have experienced the post-colonial policy, built on stereotypes and distance. However, it is impossible to put forward a thesis that, in the times of real socialism, the attitudes of Poles to the disabled were significantly different than of inhabitants of other countries. Yet, they had some specificity typical of monocultural communities. It can be described in:

- negative categories – ignorance, fear, pity, passiveness, creating a distance;
- positive categories – interest, solidarity.

Rooting the way of thinking about the disabled in particular categories is determined by: family and school education, experience, personality traits and the local attitude, also the one presented in media. What seemed a major burden in the views on disabled people in the discussed period was attributing stereotypical and limiting social roles to them. However, this was a characteristic feature of many other societies as well.

The circumstances determining monoculturalism started to change alongside the increasing economic migration after 1989 and higher living standards of Poles, which enhanced tourism. Currently, economic migration to Poland can be observed, especially from Asian and East-European countries (especially Ukraine). These experiences are favourable for creating cultural borderlands and are a challenge for school education. Unfortunately, growing multiculturalism triggers off also some nationalist attitudes, typical of extreme right-wing social movements (Nikitorowicz, 2017). Luckily, they are not common, even though they comply with the government's conservative policy towards immigrants.

Assuming that the culture of inclusion increases in direct proportion to cultural diversification, a thesis can be put forward that these changes enhance the inclusion of disabled people. The analysis of numerous studies on the social distance and attitudes to people with disability shows differentiated results (Ostrowska, 1997; Chodkowska, Kazanowski, 2007; Kirenko, 2007; Kazanowski, 2011; Ćwirynkało, 2010; Sękowski, Zieliński, 2010; Chodkowska, Szabała, 2012; Pielecki, 2013; Kirenko, Wawer, 2015). They are determined by many variables. The major ones are the type and the degree of disability. Most frequently, the studies reveal a bigger distance and more ambivalent attitudes to the intellectually disabled than to people with sensory and motoric disorders. Another factor which differentiates attitudes is the respondents' level of education – higher education enhances the declarations of openness to unlikeness and its acceptance. The respondents' age is a very important differentiating variable. A comprehensive analysis of the Polish research into the attitudes to the disabled in various periods of life (pre-school, school and university age, adulthood) has been presented by Iwona Chrzanowska (2015, pp. 98–120). In her opinion, the attitudes at pre-school and school age are characterized by a low level of acceptance, the declarations of contacts and of knowledge concerning disability. Favourable attitudes are more often declared by university students and adults, although they are also differentiated, depending on the examined (cognitive, emotional, behavioural) component.

Comparative studies do not indicate significant differences between the attitudes of Poles and other nations (Bera, Korczyński, 2012; Gajdzica, 2013).

Distance and limited readiness to work with a disabled learner in mainstream school are declared by the majority of teachers (Pielecki, Kazanowski, 2001; Jachimczak, 2008; Chrzanowska, 2014; Gajdzica, 2011; Skibska, 2016). Yet, the analysis of the research results show that these attitudes are slowly changing towards acceptance and readiness for inclusive education.

To sum up, it is difficult to reach an unambiguous opinion on the discussed issue. Although the analysis shows a tendency to change towards acceptance and shortening the distance to people with disabilities, these tendencies are not unambiguous in all areas. What should be emphasized in this context is the political distance and lack of social needs necessary for the broadly understood educational inclusion associated with cultural diversity. In Poland, this seems to be one of the reasons of the development of inclusion written into the tradition of special education and, at the same time, the marginalization of the current based on its deconstruction.

1.2. Inclusive education in practice

1.2.1. Organization of inclusive education

Educating learners with special educational needs in Poland is regulated by many legal documents at the level of directives. Among other things, they concern: the conditions of organizing such education (Directive of the Ministry of National Education of 24th July, 2015), certificates and opinions provided by psychological-pedagogical counselling centres (Directive of the Ministry of National Education of 18th September, 2008), organizing psychological-pedagogical support (Directive of the Ministry of National Education of 30th April, 2013), financial aspects (Directive of the Ministry of National Education of 20th March, 2018) and several other issues comprised in acts pertaining to broadly understood education and care for all learners. The acts are altered very often. Thus, an average teacher or even a kindergarten or school head-teacher can have serious problems with their detailed analysis. This is difficult because the regulations concerning disabled learners are comprised also in some general acts. The detailed discussion of the regulations will be omitted here in favour of most important general issues.

After the diagnosis in the psychological-pedagogical counselling centre and obtaining by the learner a certificate concerning the need of special education (e.g. due to disability), parents choose the form of education. The following forms are possible:

- special (special school or special class in mainstream school),
- integrated (integrated school or integrated class in mainstream school),
- inclusive (mainstream school).

In some justified cases, the counselling centre can issue an opinion recommending individual teaching at the learner's home (until 2017 it was also possible at school).

The choice of a particular school is always made by parents – the head-teacher has to admit a learner with disability if the school is in the learner's educational district.

In Poland, inclusive education can take place in all widely accessible educational institutions. There are no acts which limit or favour certain institutions. This does not mean that all mainstream kindergartens and schools have similar conditions for educating disabled learners.

Mainstream kindergartens and schools:

- have to employ assistants only for learners with some selected disabilities (Asperger's syndrome, autism, multiple disabilities);

- have to prepare the Individual Educational-Therapeutic Syllabus (IETS) for each learner with disability. It is elaborated by a team appointed by the head-teacher. IETS comprises:
  - the scope and way of adjusting the educational requirements to the learner's individual needs and psycho-physical potentialities,
  - suggestions for integrating activities of teachers and specialists,
  - the forms and period of providing psychological-pedagogical support for the learner,
  - parental support activities,
  - revalidation and socio-therapeutic classes,
  - various activities concerning career counselling,
  - the scope of collaboration of teachers and specialists with the learner's parents in the implementation of the regulations comprised in the document certifying the need for special education;
- have to ensure that each learner with disability takes part in at least two hours of additional revalidation (therapy) classes;
- treat all other forms of support as not obligatory. They depend on IETS. A disabled learner can obtain other types of support. Their range and type is determined by the local authorities financing the school (these are other additional classes, additional specialists, smaller groups, the teacher's additional qualifications in the field of educating learners with SEN).

Most of the disabled learners fulfil the core curriculum in the form of a modified educational syllabus. There is one exception – learners with profound intellectual disability, for whom the special core curriculum has been elaborated. The modifications of the curriculum are specified in the IETS in a general way and their details are provided by teachers at conducted classes. The modifications usually pertain to:

- omitting certain curricular contents and replacing them with others or simplifying them (typical in the case of learners with mild intellectual disability);
- changes in the forms of presenting the contents (most frequently in the case of learners with sensory disorders);
- portioning the contents into smaller information chunks.

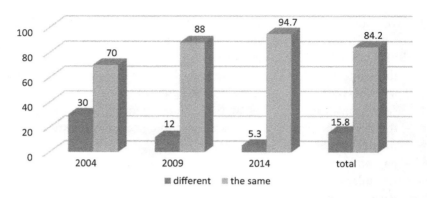

Figure 1. The coursebook used for work with a learner with mild intellectual disability (%) N=450 (source: Gajdzica, 2020)

Most frequently, teachers make use of general curricula and they adjust the implementation to the potentialities and needs of learners with disabilities. The issue of coursebooks is solved in a similar way. Even though some coursebooks for learners with SEN have been elaborated in Poland, the majority of teachers in mainstream schools use general coursebooks. As the results of some longitudinal studies show (see Figure 1), in inclusive education of learners with mild intellectual disability, teachers use the special coursebook for this group of learners less and less frequently in favour of the general coursebook.[3] This enhances the socialization of disabled children in class but often lowers the quality of their education.

The number of learners educated in integrated and mainstream classes has been steadily growing for several years. Yet, the number of learners in special schools has been decreasing. This is illustrated by the data on primary schools presented in Table 2. In the early 1990s, there were no statistics in Poland concerning the number of disabled learners in mainstream

---

3   This is a section of the unpublished results of the research project entitled "Uczeń z lekką niepełnosprawnością intelektualną w klasie ogólnodostępnej [A learner with mild intellectual disability in the mainstream class]." The studies were conducted among 450 mainstream school teachers who educated learners with mild intellectual disability in their classes in three time periods – 2004 / 2009 / 2014.

Table 2. Students with special educational needs in primary schools for children and youth (source: Oświata i wychowanie w roku szkolnym 2016 / 17, p. 144)

School year	Form of organization			
	special primary school	special group in primary school	integrated group in primary school	mainstream group in primary school
1990/1991	84 317	17 363	-	-
1995/1996	82 999	6 613	2 036	4 158
2000/2001	52 020	3 207	6 897	37 890
2010/2011	24 459	1 725	14 539	20 488
2014/2015	23 577	857	14 652	23 944
2016/2017	24 298	967	16 491	31 555

classes. These statistics started to be recorded several years later, though they were not fully reliable. Therefore, the number of disabled learners in mainstream classes was understated in the data from the school year 1995/96. The 2000/2001 data shows already a high percentage of learners with disabilities educated in natural inclusion – at that time, still with very limited support. What draws attention is a rapid decrease in the number of learners educated in special classes in mainstream schools. While analysing the data, it should be remembered that the number of all learners (also disabled ones) has decreased in Poland. However, it has grown in the case of some disabilities – for instance, the number of learners with autism has increased ten times over the last decade (System Informacji Oświatowej [System of Educational Information], 2018).

Similar changes have occurred in education for the disabled in lower-secondary schools (see: Table 3). Lower-secondary schools were introduced into the Polish system of education by the reform in 1999. Currently, due to another reform, they are being phased out and the return to the former eight class primary school is taking place.

In the school year 2016/2017, 73.3 thousand learners with special educational needs were educated in primary schools for children and youth, out of whom 24.0 thousand were girls. They constituted 3.2 % of the total number of learners in these schools. The highest percentage in the group of disabled learners was of learners with mild intellectual disability (25.1 %), multiple disabilities (18.7 %), autism – including Asperger's

Table 3. Students with special educational needs in lower secondary schools for children and youth (source: Oświata i wychowanie w roku szkolnym 2016 / 17, p. 147)

School year	Form of organization			
	special lower secondary school	special group in lower secondary school	integrated group in lower secondary school	mainstream group in lower secondary school
2000/2001	30 367	1 672	1 109	15 432
2005/2006	35 649	1 813	5 225	21 388
2010/2011	29 733	1 826	7 811	14 586
2014/2015	25 125	679	7 014	14 386
2016/2017	23 190	569	7 585	16 096

syndrome (16.2 %), motor disability – including aphasia (11.6 %) and moderate or severe intellectual disability (11.1 %). 24.3 thousand learners with SEN attended 794 primary schools. Most of them were located in the Masovian (120 schools), Silesian (89 schools) and Lower Silesian (82 schools) Voivodeships. Boys significantly prevailed in these schools – there were 50 girls per 100 boys. The number of special primary schools is much bigger in towns than in villages. This results from the activity of psychological-pedagogical counselling centres and other institutions providing support for the disabled and acting for their integration with the environment (Oświata i wychowanie w roku szkolnym 2016 / 17, p. 92).

In the school year 2016/2017, 47.7 thousand learners with SEN attended lower-secondary schools for children and youth, out of whom 17 thousand were girls. Learners with SEN constituted 4.5 % (as in the previous school year) of the total number of learners in lower-secondary schools for children and youth. 51.1 % of all learners with SEN attended mainstream lower-secondary schools – 2.2 % more than in the previous school year. Among disabled learners educated in special and mainstream lower-secondary schools, the biggest number was of learners with mild intellectual disability (15.3 thousand), moderate or severe intellectual disability (6.7 thousand), multiple disabilities (6.6 thousand) and learners endangered with social maladjustment (5.7 thousand). The number of learners with other disabilities was 13.6 thousand.

23.2 thousand learners with special educational needs attended 847 special lower-secondary schools – 48.9 % of all learners with SEN, 2.2 % fewer than in the previous school year. The largest number of special lower-secondary schools were located in the Masovian (131 schools), Lower Silesian (98 schools) and Silesian (88 schools) Voivodeships. Boys attending these schools outnumbered girls. In 2016/2017, there were 56 girls per 100 boys. The number of special lower-secondary schools is bigger in towns than in villages. As in the case of primary education, this is associated with the location of psychological-pedagogical counselling centres and other institutions providing support for the disabled and acting for their integration with the environment (Oświata i wychowanie w roku szkolnym 2016 / 17, pp. 93–94).

In general, openness is a characteristic feature of the Polish system of education. It enables horizontal patency – changing the educational institution at any period of education. In practice, this usually consists in changing mainstream school for integrated or special school. The reversed changes take place very rarely (Grzyb, 2013). Schools do not need to fulfil many legal requirements to conduct inclusive education, teachers do not need to be especially prepared. Yet, apart from the obligatory support, a learner with SEN can get additional aid, which depends on the decision of the local authorities.

The analysis of legal transformations in the field of education for learners with SEN in recent decades allows for distinguishing several tendencies. The major ones involve:

- including possibly the biggest number of learners with SEN into obligatory school education and providing intensive support for them;
- creating possibly the best conditions for integrated and inclusive education;
- creating the space for the development of special education in the non-government sector.

However, it is impossible to recognize these tendencies as a mature strategy, showing a map of beneficial (necessary and feasible) changes. In fact, most of the changes concern fragmentary (not always coherent) modernization of some elements of the special education system and favouring some particular ideologies (as a result of creating disharmonious conditions for the development of particular forms of education and their stages). The lack of a transparent strategy surely enhances the creation of the fictitious reality associated with excessive legal regulation of the applied solutions and the need of documenting them in daily educational practice (Gajdzica, 2016). Nevertheless, this policy along with social transformations is favourable for statistical changes in the field of education for learners with disabilities. The changes clearly show an increase in the number of disabled learners fulfilling the school duty in integrated and mainstream institutions. Thus, it can be stated that the system of separated education is systematically evolving towards inclusive education.

1.2.2. Financing the education of learners with disabilities

The organization of education for learners with disabilities is the responsibility of territorial authorities. Kindergartens, primary and lower-secondary mainstream schools (also with integrated classes) are most frequently run by municipalities (the lowest administrative levels). Special schools are usually run by counties (the middle level) and voivodeships. As a rule, counties are also responsible for upper-secondary mainstream schools.

Financial resources for the implementation of educational tasks are given to local authorities in the form of educational subvention. Every year, the Minister of National Education (in a directive) announces the amount of the subvention per a learner. In the recent years, it has increased insignificantly in relation to inflation, e.g. In the recent years, it has increased insignificantly in relation to inflation, e.g. in 2011 it was 4 364 PLN (about 980 EUR), in 2014 – 5 242 PLN (about 1 190 EUR), and in 2017 – 5 331 PLN (about 1 210 EUR).

The amount of additional resources is related to the learner's disability. The annual directives of the Minister of National Education specify the ranks (multipliers) which indicate how the basic rate per a learner will be multiplied (Annex to the Directive of the Ministry of National Education of 18th December 2013 on the allocation of partial educational subvention for units of territorial authorities in 2014).

For instance, the algorithm for 2014 takes into consideration 45 ranks. Four of them concern disabled learners, two – disabled children educated in kindergartens. Some sample algorithms are provided below:

P2 = 1.40 for learners with mild intellectual disability, social maladjustment, behaviour disorders, learners endangered with addiction or social
maladjustment, learners with chronic diseases – requiring the application of special organization of education and methods of work.

P3 = 2.90 for sightless and visually impaired learners, learners with motor
disability (including aphasia), learners with mental disorders – requiring
the application of special organization of education and methods
of work.

P4 = 3.60 for deaf learners, learners with hearing impairment, learners
with moderate or severe intellectual disability.

P5 = 9.50 for children and youth with severe intellectual disability, fulfilling school obligation by participation in revalidation-educational
classes organized by primary and lower-secondary schools, for learners
with multiple disabilities and autism (including Asperger's syndrome).

P32 = 4.00 for deaf or aurally impaired learners, blind or visually impaired
learners, learners with motor disability (including aphasia), learners
with mild, moderate, severe and profound intellectual disability –
included into special education in kindergartens, kindergarten groups
organized in primary schools, other forms of pre-school education, as
well as children in special kindergartens and kindergarten groups in
special primary schools organized within health care institutions.

P40 = 9.50 for learners from revalidation-educational centres and children
with multiple disabilities and autism (including Asperger's syndrome)
who are educated in kindergartens, kindergarten groups organized in
primary schools, and in other forms of pre-school education.

This apparently well-organized and beneficial (for disabled learners)
system has one fundamental drawback – transferring the money for every
learner to local authorities, which include it into the general educational
budget. Then, this budget is distributed to particular schools under their
charge. At this stage, this money gets mixed with other educational funds
and it does not have to be dedicated entirely to the education of a particular learner (Waszkiewicz, Dumnicka, 2012). They might be used to
pay for e.g. heating, teaching aids for the whole school, organization of
sport competitions. The situation is better in the case of private educational institutions (e.g. run by associations), which get the whole of the

subvention. It is one of the reasons for the recent increase in their number – especially of those institutions which educate learners with more profound deficiencies as in their case the ranks are the highest. For instance, the annual subvention for children and youth with profound intellectual disability in 2017 was: 5 331 x 9.5 = 50 644 PLN (about 11 610 EUR). In Polish conditions, this is a high amount which can entirely fulfil the educational and care needs of a learner with profound intellectual disability. What seems a weakness of this system is the underfinancing of learners with less serious disabilities. To exemplify this, in 2017 local authorities received for a learner with mild intellectual disability 5 331 x 1.4 = 7 643.4 PLN (about 1 711 EUR). This sum is not sufficient to organize well-developed support for this group of learners. Therefore, special and integrated education of learners with less serious disabilities is often subsidized from the own resources of local governments. Private institutions educating learners with less serious disabilities are rather rare – this is a sector that hardly exists in Poland.

However, it is worth noticing that this mechanism facilitates educational inclusion of learners with less serious disabilities. As mentioned earlier, inclusive education in Poland does not demand many formal requirements, therefore – it is not expensive. Therefore, local governments aim at the largest number of learners with mild disability fulfilling their educational duty in mainstream institutions.

1.2.3. Competences and qualifications of teachers in inclusive education

The introduction of educational inclusion (treated as a new form of teaching based on the Copernican turn of the present education) is an enormous challenge for the whole system of education. It requires a fundamental change of the organizational culture of school.

Changing the culture of school may take place on the basis of:

• transformations of knowledge – the suppression of the old knowledge by the new one, in this case – the new knowledge which constitutes the ideological foundation of inclusive school. This knowledge gives particular meanings to everyday events at school. It focuses on the assumptions of: the relations between school and the environment, the

nature of human activities, the truth and time, the human nature, inter-personal relations (Tuohy, 2002, pp. 25–26);
• understanding and acceptance of the need for transformations, expressed by the head-teacher, teachers and – to a smaller extent – by parents and learners.

Among other things, this is the reason why teachers' competences cannot be discussed quite apart from their attitudes and readiness for change. In other words, the readiness for change is a kind of competence, which – in the discussed case – determines successful transformations of the culture of school much more than teachers' expert and methodolog-ical competences.

Thus, it is not surprising that in Poland, similarly to other countries, the studies on teachers' attitudes to inclusive education and their readiness for including disabled learners attract a lot of research focus. In recent years, these attitudes have not significantly evolved towards higher acceptance of educational inclusion. Most of the surveyed teachers in mainstream schools present negative or ambivalent attitudes. The studies conducted by Krystyna Błeszyńska (1992) in the early 1990s indicated that 85 % of teachers in mainstream schools would not take on a disabled learner in their class if they could decide. Urszula Bartnikowska and Marta Wójcik (2004) in their research showed that only 26 % of the surveyed teachers from mainstream schools educating children with hearing impairment had undertaken that task of their own free will – for the rest, it had been imposed. The studies carried out in 2011 indicated that as many as 85 % of the examined teachers from mainstream schools expressed their objection to inclusive education of learners with mild intellectual disability (Gajdzica, 2011).

Teachers differentiate their attitudes depending on the type of the learner's disability. The smallest chance for acceptance in the process of inclusion is in the case of learners with intellectual and motor disability, the biggest – with sensory disorders (Pielecki, Kazanowski, 2001).

It is assumed in this study that a teacher's professional competences are a set of professional skills and dispositions which constitute the equipment of an educator. They are necessary to work effectively (Průcha, Walterovà, Mareš, 2003, p. 104). These competences are in fact the teacher's abilities and readiness to do tasks at the expected level. They result from integrating the knowledge – numerous minor skills and abilities related to selection and evaluation. They are often considered to be an effect of the educational process (Kwiatkowska, 2008). Competences are subject-oriented and dynamic. Therefore, there are no competences acquired and consolidated once and forever. They are a function of time and professional activeness of the subject (Dudzikowa, 1994). They are also viewed as the adaptational or transgressive potential of the teacher. In the first case, they allow for adjusting the subject's activities to the surrounding environment, treated as a static reality. This concept, grounded in the behaviouristic perspective, indicates the instrumental character of these activities, because it is a directive to instrumental acting aimed at fulfilling a particular goal. The second concept appears as the transgressive potential of the subject, in which the generated types of activities are prone to creative modification. This modification becomes real as a result of interpretation as long as the dynamic context of acting is assumed. With this assumption, competences are a type of deep cognitive structure which integrates its functional elements and counterbalances human relations with the world (Męczkowska, 2003). There are many classifications of competences. For the needs of this study – in reference to the competences of teachers from inclusive mainstream schools, they can be divided into:

- humanistic – the general knowledge of social processes, culture and the development of civilization;
- general pedagogical – the general knowledge of pedagogy and psychology, the skills of working with a group, the skills of designing and implementing the educational process;
- content-based – the knowledge of the taught subject, methodological skills of teaching this subject;
- specialist competences – the knowledge of developmental disorders, disabilities, methodological skills needed for work with learners with SEN.

In Poland, teachers in mainstream schools do not need to document their special qualifications (also competences) to work with disabled learners. Most of the teachers of particular subjects acquire their teaching qualifications during a short university course within their studies (it used to be about 350 hours) or lifelong learning (courses – 270 hours, postgraduate studies – 350 hours). While acquiring these qualifications, they do not have classes in pedagogy and psychology of disability at all or have hardly any. Therefore, teachers' reluctant attitudes to educational inclusion should not surprise. The majority of teachers of subjects face a learner with SEN no sooner than in their professional work – they fulfil the special or specially tailored curriculum in an intuitive way. In 2011, some obligatory contents (in a scarce range) concerning the learner with SEN appeared obligatorily within curricula for teachers. In the case of early education teachers, the situation is slightly better. During their studies, they usually fulfil the course of special education and the elements of clinical psychology. Yet, these classes provide only the minimum of the knowledge pertaining to disability. Moreover, they usually take place without practical internships. Some positive changes take place in the field of lifelong learning. A growing number of primary school teachers do courses and post-graduate studies in education of learners with SEN.

These changes are reflected in the results of the tracking studies among teachers from mainstream schools conducting inclusive education for learners with mild intellectual disability (Figure 2).

The presented data concern mainstream school teachers who work at least with one learner with mild intellectual disability. The data analysis shows that in 1999 the vast majority of surveyed teachers declared the

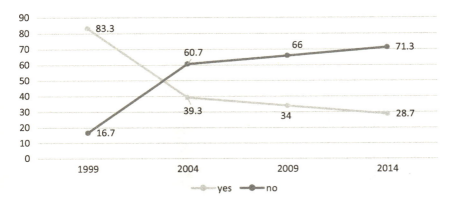

Figure 2. Declared completion of post-graduate studies or a course in the field of work with a disabled learner (including the 1999 data) N=653 (source: Gajdzica, 2020)

lack of education in the field of competences in special pedagogy. The most dynamic increase in the acquisition of these competences took place just after the introduction of the in-depth educational reform in 1999. It emphasized the development of integrated education, which might have been one of the enhancers of such enormous popularity of training in special education. What is observed later is the continuous (though less dynamic) growth of the number of mainstream teachers undertaking additional training in the work with learners with SEN. However, these results cannot be generalized into the whole population – also to the teachers who do not work with disabled learners in mainstream school. It is worth reminding that in the 1990s, similarly to the present day, work with a disabled learner in mainstream school did not necessitate the acquisition of qualifications in special education. Courses and studies, as forms of lifelong learning, most frequently require fees. As this training is undertaken mostly on teachers' own initiative, its costs are rarely refunded. Unfortunately, post-graduate studies and qualification courses are conducted by many various institutions and, therefore, they do not always provide high quality.

In Figure 3, the results are presented of the declarations provided by mainstream school teachers, concerning their subjective feeling of being prepared for work with a learner with mild intellectual disability. The declarations indicate a systematic increase in positive opinions.

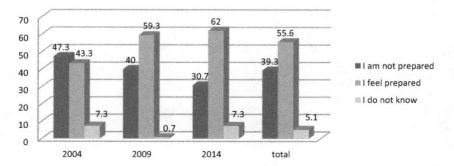

Figure 3. Subjective feeling of teachers' preparation for work with a learner with mild intellectual disability (%) (N=450) (source: Gajdzica, 2020)

Similar results were obtained in the studies by Anna Zamkowska (2009, p. 207). She conducted her research among teachers of early school education in mainstream schools, also those who had undertaken inclusion of learners with mild intellectual disability. Her research results show that over 60 % of the respondents assess their knowledge concerning work with learners with SEN as rather good and not even 25 % as insufficient (Zamkowska, 2009, p. 207). Yet, Ewa Kochanowska has received slightly more pessimistic results in the discussed field – over 60 % of early school education teachers defined their preparation as insufficient (Kochanowska, 2015, pp. 150–151).

Although teachers' subjective feelings are not an objectivized indicator of their real competences in the discussed area, they reflect their mindset (the emotional component of an attitude) concerning inclusive education. In other words – teachers who negatively assess their competences to work with learners with SEN usually manifest their distance to educational inclusion. Their characteristic feature is resistance to change. This interrelation was confirmed still in the 1990s by Elżbieta Minczakiewicz (1996).

Summing up, mainstream school teachers working with learners with SEN do not have specialist competences. Unfortunately, the current system of acquiring teaching qualifications does not take into account competences to work with disabled learners or considers them in a very small extent. Most probably, this is one of the reasons of not very favourable attitudes of teachers to inclusive education and their lack of readiness for the inclusion of disabled learners. A new act changing the contents of education for future teachers is being prepared now. This project takes into consideration the basic knowledge of learners' disability and the rudiments of educating the disabled.

1.2.4. Principles of work in the inclusive class

The principles of work in the inclusive class are strictly related to the applied concept of inclusive education. As mentioned earlier, there are two possible standpoints:

- the first is based on viewing educational inclusion as the continuation (development) of special and integrated education. This is the dominating current in the Polish thinking about educational inclusion of

learners with disability. In this approach, the rules formed on the basis of special education are a starting point for the conceptualization of methodology but they undergo some modifications;
- the second presents educational inclusion as a new form of education, unrelated to special education and even built on its deconstruction. This approach requires creating the methodology of inclusive education without reaching for the principles elaborated in special education.

Both concepts will be discussed below with an attempt at their comparative overview. My assumption is that they form a constitutive construct in either of the concepts. However, some general references to principles in educational processes will be made at first.

Disagreement in the understanding of rules of education has intensified both the divergence in their definitions or numbers and their unchanging character. As regards their definitions, there are two basic approaches in the Polish tradition.

The first shows a principle as a statement based on scientific laws ruled by repeatability in particular conditions. In this sense, didactic principles are a type of established regularities (Okoń, 1995, pp. 167–168). This idea is based on the universality of rules. It is expressed in the assumption of certain generality or even timelessness. Applying this assumption requires the recognition of some regularities in educational processes, which brings about grounding pedagogy as a science in the positivist paradigm associated with a nomothetic explanation of didactic situations. Such an approach to principles is presented, among others, by Włodzimierz Szewczuk (1993, pp. 978–979), who claims that the rules of education express objective regularities, they depend neither on the learner's personality nor on the educational system, and their number should reflect the revealed rules of educational activities. What seems worth adding is that Szewczuk objects to separating the didactic rules from rules of moral education. He claims that some particular rules of learning – which constitute the common thread – make the foundation for the acquisition of knowledge, its processing and working out the ways of conduct.

Compliantly with the second sense, principles are the norms of conduct recognized as appropriate (favourable). They are established intuitively and obeying them should be obligatory during the course of education

(Okoń, 1995, p. 168). The analysis of didactic literature shows that this understanding of rules is the most popular in Poland. This understanding is based on treating the rules as the norms of conduct which is:

- recognized as appropriate (optimal) for fulfilling the established goals;
- changeable in particular didactic-educational situations;
- a regulator of the conduct of teachers and learners in the educational process (Półturzycki, 1997).

This standpoint allows both for treating norms as constructs adjusted to the individual concept of teacher's work and as the foundation for the organization of methodical work in particular changeable conditions. With its clear reference to the humanistic paradigms of practicing science, this approach is compliant with the deconstructive concepts of educational inclusions (Thomas, Loxley, 2007).

Thus, it can be said that the relations of the principles of educational inclusion as a form of special education and of inclusive education as deconstruction of special education are based on the opposition of:

- principles as rules and as the norms,
- the individual and social model of disability,
- traditional (quasi-behavioural) and constructivist didactics.

In the further part, the focus will be on the principles associated with the organization of inclusive education – the principles directly associated with the learning process itself (e.g. the systemic character, perceivability, independence, the relation between theory and practice, effectiveness, gradation of difficulty, the relation between individualization and socialization) will be omitted (Okoń, 1997, p. 171).

A short description of some selected principles is presented below in the versions for both types of inclusive education. This is preceded by two tables which constitute the context for the formulated principles. The first concerns educational culture based on the individual versus social model (Table 4), the second pertains to the comparison of behavioural and constructivist didactics (Table 5). As the tables form only the background for the rules formulated below, they are not discussed separately.

The presented principles are not all the possible ones. Their choice has been based on the basic criteria differentiating the two types of inclusion.

Table 4. Educational culture based on the individual and social model (source: own elaboration with the use of the assumptions of the medical and social model of disability)

Comparison criterion	Educational culture based on the individual model of disability	Educational culture based on the social model of disability
Approach to special needs of a learner	Burden	Challenge
Source of special needs	A result of functional disorders	Inadequate expectations, lack of curricular adjustment
Essence of special needs	Difficulties in fulfilling didactic and educational goals	Searching for optimal ways of development
Scope of the phenomenon	Personal dimension	Within the organization of classroom work and the organization of school
Learner's role	A disabled learner requiring special aid	An exceptional learner requiring rational support and unique organization of the educational process
Solution	Professional intervention of specialists, individualization if possible, special aid	Education tailored to potentialities, adjustment, elimination of barriers, individualization if necessary
Control	Results of school achievements in the aspect of curricular requirements	Evaluation of progress – development of skills and competences
Expected results	Adaptation to school requirements	Acceptance of the potentialities, adjustment of expectations – change in organization

Some differences are excessively emphasized here but in educational practice they are not always so striking. It seems that the current image of the Polish inclusive practice is reflected (though not in the exact form) in the left column of the formulated principles in Table 6.

The principles formulated in the first column are based on certain fetishization of inclusion itself. This fetishization is constituted on the opposition to segregating and separating practices. In this approach, inclusive education is aimed mostly at collaboration in one main current. It is treated

Table 5. The comparison of the model of behavioural and constructivist didactics (source: Klus-Stańska, 2010, p. 342)

Elements of didactics	Quasi-behavioural didactics	Constructivist didactics
Subject of learning	Notions and instructions	Meanings, individualized cognitive representations and strategies
Source of knowledge	Public "objective" findings	Cognitive conflict
Essence of teaching	Transmission of notions	Organization of conditions for learning
Essence of learning	Acquisition of notions	Negotiating, constructing and attributing the meanings
Assumed relation between teaching and learning	Compatibility, tight relations	No compatibility, questionable relations (teaching as inspiration)
Educational goals	Standardized result (process as a tool)	Diversified processes (result as a derivate)
Teacher's role	Specialist, organizer, companion	Organizer, negotiator, companion
Learner's role	Recipient	Creator
Function of personal knowledge	Secondary, disturbing	Fundamental, examined by the teacher and learner
Essence of good activeness	Industriousness, guided participation	Conceptual independence, cognitive responsibility
Planning	Strict	Approximate, framework-based
Control	Measurement or description of the result, diagnosis of the deficiency	Description of cognitive procedures, diagnosis of progress

as a certain model and a reference point for other activities. This concept can be justified due to its low level of heterogeneity in class groups. It should be remembered that cultural diversification in Poland is still slight and the practices in noticing other differences are rather modest as well. As a result, educational inclusion is usually understood as including one or two learners (differing in some particular scopes) into the class group which is viewed as homogeneous. This is illustrated in Table 7, in which the practices are presented in the organization of didactic situations in the class with one disabled learner.

Table 6. Selected principles of two types of inclusive education (source: Gajdzica, 2019, p. 36)

The principle pertaining to:	Educational inclusion of disabled learners as a form of continuation of special education	Educational inclusion of disabled learners as a form of deconstruction of special education
the current	There is the main current of a lesson. It constitutes the centre for organizing lesson work. It is a kind of organizational model of lessons. Collateral currents appear in the course of individualization. They are subordinated to the main current.	Many parallel, symmetrical and asymmetrical, currents are constructed. They are not complementary with each other. There might not (though there can) exist one main organizational current which is a reference point for all activities.
developmental goals	Equipping the learner with the knowledge and skills which will enable the implementation of the core curriculum.	The learner's development. Equipping learners with the knowledge and skills which will enable them to acquire social competences and to fulfil developmental tasks in compliance with their potentialities.
organizational goals	Inclusion into the mainstream of all learners if only possible	Creating currents tailored to every learner. If possible, they can be merged into one broader current.
space	There is the main space, which constitutes the centre of "what is happening in class." Collateral spaces come into being through individualization of selected learners.	There is one main space. It is not reserved only for joint activities.
the teacher's time	Distribution of time in opposition to activities in the mainstream and collateral currents	Distribution of time without opposition.
diversity	Aimed at including into the area of the defined norm – standardization according to a particular model. The model is defined by the possibility to implement the general core curriculum.	Treating diversity as the norm. Activities aimed at standardization appear only in the scope of fulfilling common developmental needs.
adjustment in fulfilling educational tasks	First of all aimed at a learner, secondly – at a change of learning conditions	No adjustment activities, activities aimed at a change of learning conditions in the case of fulfilling joint educational tasks.
activities	Distribution of activities in the main and collateral currents based on opposition.	All activities in different currents. They are not comparable.

Table 7. The goals and procedures of achieving them in integrated education (source: Gajdzica, 2011, p. 127)

Procedures of achieving goals / Goals	Identical for all learners	Partially different for a learner with disability	Different for a learner with disability
Identical for all learners	A. 1. Work with the use of identical method, means and organizational forms, aimed at achieving the same goals	A2. Applying partially diversified procedures for achieving partially different goals	A3. Applying different procedures for achieving identical goals
Partially different for a learner with disability	B.1. Work with the use of identical procedures aimed at achieving partially different goals	B.2. Applying partially diversified procedures for achieving partially different goals	B.3. Applying different procedures for achieving partially different goals
Different for a learner with disability	C.1. Work with the use of identical procedures aimed at achieving totally different goals	C.2. Applying partially diversified procedures for achieving totally different goals	C.3. Applying diversified procedures for achieving totally different goals

This table clearly refers to the organization of inclusive education based on the reconstruction of the assumptions of special education. In simpler terms – a learner with disability can fulfil common, partially common or different goals at which other learners aim. The same distinction pertains to procedures – to the applied methods, didactic means, organizational forms and educational contents. From the standpoint of inclusive effectiveness, the most beneficial model is A1, in which a learner with disability achieves the same goals as other learners by learning in the same way. Obviously, this is not always feasible in practice. Therefore, many indirect organizational forms come into being. They are associated with the modification of goals and/or organizational activities. Every modification requires a certain degree of individualization. Thus, in practice – this necessitates the creation of an additional collateral educational current. Its most explicit form is the situation reflected by model C3. As a result of such organization, a disabled learner works individually for the whole lesson, fulfilling individual goals.

Summing up, the principles of inclusive education result from a particular organizational culture of inclusion. This culture is determined by both the perception of disability (as an objectively existing feature or a feature constructed / revealed in some particular conditions) and the relation to special education (to the reconstruction or deconstruction of its assumptions).

1.2.5. Barriers to the development of inclusive education

The barriers for the development of inclusive education can be divided into:

- mental barriers – associated with unfavourable attitudes to people with disability;
- organizational-institutional barriers – related to the lack of preparation of school and the local community. Within this field, the following can be distinguished:
  - legal barriers – originating from irrational solutions necessitated or promoted by particular regulations in legal acts;
  - economic barriers – resulting from insufficient financial resources, required for full participation of learners with disability in the system of education.

The barriers in human minds seem the most difficult to eliminate. In the case of the approach to inclusive education, they are associated with unfavourable attitudes to the disabled.

In compliance with the theory of tripartite structure of the attitude, the sources of barriers can be sought in three components. The first is the lack of knowledge (or the beliefs consolidated on false or colloquial knowledge) concerning: the needs and potentialities of disabled learners, the organizational possibilities of the educational system, the effectiveness of inclusive education. The lack of knowledge is the foundation of unfavourable mental outlooks. This is the second component of the attitude, rooted in the emotional sphere. Among its characteristic features, there is the unwillingness to joint education of learners with and without disability. These attitudes come into being due to:

- stereotypes – in this approach they mostly concern parents who feel that their children's safety may be endangered;

- the reluctance towards changes and the related difficulties – in this area they mostly concern teachers who experience a fear of difficulties associated with ensuring the best learning conditions for all learners in a class;
- the belief that disabled learners have too many conveniences in comparison to other learners' needs, which are fulfilled in a limited way.

The third component is the lack of activities for the object of the attitude. Here, this means not undertaking any activities aimed at educational inclusion – the passiveness concerning promoting it, preparing the conditions and implementing it in practice.

Organizational-institutional barriers can be divided into individual (pertaining to one institution) and systemic ones. The former result from the hermetic institutional knowledge which a particular school has. Institutional knowledge comprises the elements of both the colloquial and scientific knowledge. Its characteristic quality is sharing the knowledge (by the members of an institution) of the regulations concerning the own role and other social roles in this institution. This knowledge is universally accepted by the members, it does not need justification and is not subjected to any processing by its users. Knowledge understood in this way imposes certain inflexibility of conduct and necessitates the adjustment to the binding rules. However, it does not imply the users' necessity to identify with it (Kowalik, 1989, pp. 7–8). Eclecticism of this set of knowledge can be clearly seen – it is manifested in the acceptance of both contradicting, incomplete information, often without a context or scientifically confirmed information, obtained in compliance with scientifically recognized rules. However, what seems important is that this knowledge is widely accepted within the institution, it is considered valuable and usually compatible with the interest of the institution. This knowledge is generated in the interaction of the members of the institution and their common interests. In the discussed case, it is expressed by general unwillingness to inclusion and a fear of change felt at school. It frequently results from the lack of preparation of a particular institution in regard to physical space (architectural barriers, no didactic aids, no appropriate classrooms for work with heterogeneous groups) or from the earlier discussed individual attitudes of teachers and parents, which are shared by the majority of teachers and are perpetuated in mutual interactions.

As regards systemic barriers, the inappropriate preparation of teachers (discussed here earlier) seems the most frequent one. This involves insufficient knowledge and skills needed in work with groups which are diverse and differ in the potentialities concerning the implementation of the curriculum. Other systemic barriers are related to the lack of appropriate legal regulations associated with broader (usually more expensive) support and to ignoring the need for proper inclusive competences of teachers. This involves the permanent lack of assistants, the lack of appropriate physical conditions (architectural barriers, inadequate space management) as well as too many learners in a class. The last two elements are typical legal and economic barriers.

In general, the indicated barriers bring about insufficient culture of (both organizational and mental) inclusion.

1.2.6. Developmental prospects of inclusive education

The advancement of inclusive education is a natural consequence of social, political and educational changes. Therefore, it seems that the initiated process of transformations towards the broadly understood inclusion cannot be reversed. Viewing inclusion from a broader perspective, two important threats should be mentioned. The first can be called the inner threat. This is, first of all, the affirmation of inclusion itself and treating it as a remedy for all problems (Furedi, 2008, pp. 111–114). Social / educational inclusion is not an aim itself. It is a means for achieving the aim of improved quality of life of disfavoured people and of creating the optimal conditions for their possibly fullest development. These activities are aimed at the feeling of happiness and life satisfaction of every included person. From the standpoint of social interest, the task of inclusion is to create the circumstances in which every person will be socially valuable and their potentialities will be used (with their approval) in building the community for all. The second threat of inclusion, viewed by me as external, is the inhibition or reversion of democratization processes. The assumptions of inclusion are compliant with the foundations of the democratic social order, based on the orientation towards the individual, legal equality, participation in social goods, and counteracting exclusion. Political transformations aimed at the appropriation of social space by certain groups mean – at the same time – pushing other groups into the margin of social functioning. It can be said that the return to authoritarian social and economic practices is not favourable for the development of social inclusion. In other words – it enhances the marginalization of people who do not share the ideas of the ruling authorities or, for various reasons, are not a part of the promoted (by these authorities) programme of building the community. It seems that such a situation is taking place in Poland now. Not going into the discussion on current transformations, it is enough to mention that the ruling authorities promote "the only right values" as well as being closed to otherness. This is manifested in the immigration policy, growing hostility towards strangers or in the preference of separating practices in education. These changes blow apart the foundations of the idea of inclusive culture of school. They lead to the instrumentalization of teachers (also of the institution of school) as executors of politically established directives aimed at fulfilling the needs of the ruling group. In fact, it is school and its inclusive practices which should create the open, just and participating society.

In the case of educational inclusion, there are still many threats posed by the organization of the educational system. They derive from the earlier described barriers. Therefore, the development of inclusive education for learners with disability is associated with the elimination of these barriers.

In my opinion, a lot has been done over the last two decades for the development of educational inclusion. First of all, a breakthrough has taken place in the thinking about inclusive practice as only an alternative to separated education. Its cultural and social values have been noticed as well. However, it should be kept in mind that the idea of educational inclusion in the operational dimension faces many organizational problems. In Figure 4,[4] teachers' indications of some changes in the system are presented – they are aimed at improving the conditions of inclusion.

---

4   This is a section of the unpublished results of the research project entitled "Uczeń z lekką niepełnosprawnością intelektualną w klasie ogólnodostępnej [A learner with mild intellectual disability in the mainstream class]." The studies were conducted among 450 mainstream school teachers who educated learners with mild intellectual disability in their classes in three time periods – 2005 / 2010 / 2015. Total results are presented in the figure. Each respondent could indicate any number of suggested changes.

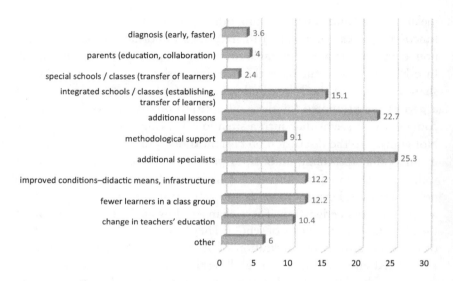

Figure 4. Teachers' suggestions for optimization of educational inclusion (source: Gajdzica, 2020)

These suggestions comply with the reconstructive model of educational inclusion. At the same time, they confirm the thesis put forward previously that this is the dominating model in the reality of Polish school. The presented suggestions show that teachers associate the improvement of inclusive conditions mostly with:

- the support of specialists dealing with education and rehabilitation of learners with disability;
- additional therapeutic and compensation classes for disabled learners;
- the development of integrated education and of the transfer of disabled learners into it, which is related to the promotion of inclusion only for selected learners.

Much less frequently, the respondents formulated indications compliant with the deconstructive model of inclusive education, associated with a change of organizational culture of school. These suggestions concerned:

- methodological support – activities aimed at improved quality of work with a diversified group in the case of professionally active teachers;

- changes in teachers' education – the problem widely discussed earlier, associated with introducing into the university curricula of pedagogical studies the contents pertaining to disability and the skills of teaching in a diversified group;
- cooperation with parents – intensification of collaboration, activation of parents in the field of implementing common educational and orgazational tasks aimed at building the organizational culture of school.

The prospects for the development of inclusive education in Poland are being shaped in an ambiguous way. On the one hand, there are the declarations of the educational authorities and their attempts to reform the system of education aimed at strengthening inclusive tendencies. On the other hand, political changes and the mentally rooted perception of inclusion in the reconstructive perspective of special pedagogy hinder the authentic construction of the inclusive culture of mainstream school.

Conclusion

Educational inclusion of learners with disability is developing dynamically in regard to statistical changes. However, this does not imply that these developmental prospects are unambiguously positive. The analysis of theoretical and practical aspects of inclusive education comprised in this chapter is my attempt to draw the research attention to the Polish reality. It largely overlaps with the educational reality of West Europe or North America, especially in the field of scientific foundations of educational practices or, partially, in teachers' education and training. The developmental ambiguity does not mean that the Polish determinants of (also inclusive) education are insignificant. On the contrary – in the case of the discussed form of education, they should be viewed as important. Some of them are rooted in the traditions of Polish education, some in the factors associated with the social and economic policy or with the social perception of the disabled. As regards inclusive education, what seems unfavourable to me are the political changes associated with drifting apart from democratic standards in educational management or with creating the social climate of the "defence" against otherness, especially in the attitudes towards immigrants. Despite many positive changes in the recent decades, another problem is the considerable insufficiency of financial resources destined for education.

Table 8. SWOT analysis of inclusive education from the standpoint of educational culture, conditions and practices (source: own studies)

Strengths	Weaknesses
• increased social awareness of the needs and potentialities of the disabled, • social acceptance of educational inclusion, • increased social awareness of parents of disabled learners, • emancipation of the environments gathering people with disabilities, • a statistical increase in the number of disabled learners educated in mainstream schools, • an increased number of mainstream school teachers with qualifications to work with learners with SEN, especially in early school education, • a growing number of scientific publications (especially conceptual considerations) on educational inclusion, • the elimination of architectural barriers in mainstream schools.	• insufficient participation of disabled learners' parents and of experts in creating the educational policy at the national and local level, • only apparent possibilities of controlling local authorities in their expenditure of additional resources for learners with certified need of special education, • insufficient competences of teachers of school subjects to work with heterogeneous groups, • teachers' ambivalent attitude to inclusive education, • teachers' mental barriers, • creating only one concept of educational inclusion based on the reconstruction of special education, • underrating the role of culture of school in creating inclusive education, • too few studies on the determinants of educational inclusion.
Opportunities	Threats
• intensifying the social activeness of the disabled, parents of disabled learners and experts in reforming the system of special education, • increasing muliculturalism of the society, • development of the concept of inclusive education based on deconstruction of special education, • changes in the education and training of mainstream school teachers – equipping them with the competences to work with diversified groups, • decreasing number of learners (birth rate drop) – resulting in smaller groups of learners, • enriching the base of didactic and methodological aids.	• political transformations – drifting apart from democratic standards (also in managing the school system), • increasing negative social attitudes to otherness, • viewing inclusion as ideology, • political tendencies towards the return to segregating practices in the educational system, • ignoring the opinions of experts and parents in building the organizational culture of inclusive school, • treating inclusive education as the cheapest form of special education.

What is presented above is my attempt to order and summarize the determinants of inclusive education. This is conducted with the use of SWOT analysis (Table 8), which also constitutes the summary of the whole chapter.

References

Apanel, D. (2016). Teoria i praktyka kształcenia integracyjnego osób z niepełnosprawnością w Polsce w latach 1989 – 2014. Kraków: Impuls.

Balcerek, M. (1981). Rozwój wychowania i kształcenia dzieci upośledzonych umysłowo. Zarys historyczny. Warszawa: WSiP.

Bartnikowska, U., Wójcik, M. (2004). *Zaniedbania w aspekcie triady: szkoła – rodzice – dziecko w kształceniu integracyjnym i masowym dzieci z wadą słuchu* (pp. 278–296). In: Z. Gajdzica, A. Klinik (Eds.), Wątki zaniedbane, zaniechane, nieobecne w procesie edukacji i wsparcia społecznego osób niepełnosprawnych. Katowice: UŚ.

Bąbka, J. (2001). Edukacja integracyjna dzieci i młodzieży pełnosprawnych i niepełnosprawnych – założenia i rzeczywistość. Poznań: Wydawnictwo Fundacji Humaniora.

Bera, R., Korczyński, M. (2012). Dystans społeczny emigrantów polskich wobec "Obcych" i "Innych." Lublin: UMCS.

Błeszyńska, K. (1992). *Determinanty przystosowania ucznia niepełnosprawnego do środowiska szkoły masowej.* In: A. Hulek, B. Grochmal-Bach (Eds.), Uczeń niepełnosprawny w szkole masowej (pp. 65–77). Kraków: WSP.

Bogucka, J., Kościelska, M. (Eds.) (1994). Wychowanie i nauczanie integracyjne. Warszawa: Centrum Metodyczne Pomocy Psychologiczno-Pedagogicznej MEN.

Bogucka, J., Kościelska, M. (Eds.) (1996). Wychowanie i nauczanie integracyjne. Nowe doświadczenia. Warszawa: Centrum Metodyczne Pomocy Psychologiczno-Pedagogicznej MEN.

Chodkowska, M., Kazanowski, Z. (2007). Socjopedagogiczne konteksty postaw nauczycieli wobec edukacji integracyjnej. Lublin: UMCS.

Chodkowska, M., Szabała, B. (2012). Osoby z upośledzeniem umysłowym w stereotypowym postrzeganiu społecznym. Lublin: UMCS.

Chrzanowska, I. (2014). Nauczanie inkluzyjne w doświadczeniach polskich – podstawy prawne i społeczne uwarunkowania. *Studia Edukacyjne*, 30, 109–117.

Chrzanowska, I. (2015). Pedagogika specjalna. Od tradycji do współczesności. Kraków: Impuls.

Cytowska, B. (2016). Przegląd empirycznych badań nad inkluzją w edukacji. *Problemy Edukacji, Rehabilitacji i Socjalizacji Osób Niepełnosprawnych*, 22, 189–213.

Czerepaniak-Walczak, M. (2015). Kultura szkoły – o jej złożoności i wielowymiarowości. *Pedagogika Społeczna*, 3 (57), 77–87.

Ćwirynkało, K. (2010). Pełnosprawni uczniowie wobec swoich rówieśników z niepełnosprawnością. *Niepełnosprawność*, 2, 93–110.

Doroszewska, J. (1989). Pedagogika specjalna. Vol. I. Podstawowe problemy teorii i praktyki. Wrocław-Kraków-Gdańsk-Łódź: Zakład Narodowy im. Ossolińskich.

Dudzikowa, M. (1994). *Kompetencje autokreacyjne – czy i jak są możliwe do nabycia w toku studiów pedagogicznych*. In: H. Kwiatkowska (Ed.), Ewolucja tożsamości pedagogiki (pp. 109–212). Warszawa: Wydawnictwo Naukowe Polskiego Towarzystwa Pedagogicznego.

Dziedzic, S. (1997). *Historia rozwoju szkolnictwa specjalnego*. In: A. Hulek (Ed.), Pedagogika rewalidacyjna (pp. 526–539). Warszawa: PWN.

Fairbairn, G., Fairbairn, S. (2000). Integracja dzieci o specjalnych potrzebach. Wybrane zagadnienia etyczne. Warszawa: Centrum Metodyczne Pomocy Psychologiczno-Pedagogicznej MEN. Original publication: Integrating Special Children: Some Ethical Issues 1998.

Firkowska-Mankiewicz, A. (2008). *Edukacja – narzędziem przeciw wykluczeniu społecznemu osób niepełnosprawnych*. In: L. Frąckiewicz (Ed.), Przeciw wykluczeniu społecznemu (pp. 224–233). Warszawa: ROPS, IPiSS.

Firkowska-Mankiewicz, A. (2012). Edukacja włączająca zadaniem dla polskiej szkoły na dziś. Warszawa: APS.

Furedi, F. (2008). Gdzie się podziali wszyscy intelektualiści, Trans. K. Makaruk. Warszawa: PIW.

References 59

Gajdzica, Z. (2010). *Codzienność ucznia niepełnosprawnego – perspektywa badawcza*. In: M. Dudzikowa. M. Czerepaniak-Walczak (Eds.), Wychowanie. Pojęcie, procesy, konteksty – interdyscyplinarne ujęcie. Vol. 5 (pp. 161–184). Gdańsk: GWP.

Gajdzica, Z. (2011). *Opinie nauczycieli szkół ogólnodostępnych na temat edukacji włączającej uczniów z lekkim upośledzeniem umysłowym w kontekście toczącej się reformy kształcenia specjalnego*. In: Z. Gajdzica (Ed.), Uczeń z niepełnosprawnością w szkole ogólnodostępnej (pp. 56–81). Sosnowiec: WSH.

Gajdzica, Z. (2011). Sytuacje trudne w opinii nauczycieli klas integracyjnych. Kraków-Katowice: Impuls-UŚ.

Gajdzica, Z. (2013). Kategorie sukcesów w opiniach nauczycieli klas integracyjnych jako przyczynek do poszukiwania koncepcji edukacji integracyjnej. Kraków-Katowice: Impuls-UŚ.

Gajdzica, Z. (2013a). Uczniowie i studenci z obszaru pogranicza wobec sytuacji osób niepełnosprawnych w środowisku lokalnym – nastawienia i opinie. Cieszyn: Stowarzyszenie Wsparcia Społecznego "Feniks."

Gajdzica, Z. (2016). Tendencje reformowania systemu kształcenia specjalnego – kilka uwag na marginesie ostatnich zmian legislacyjnych. *Niepełnosprawność. Dyskursy pedagogiki specjalnej*, 22, 39–46.

Gajdzica, Z. (2017). *Wybrane pułapki niewspółmierności w badaniach świata osób z niepełnosprawnością*. In: M. Dudzikowa, S. Juszczyk (Eds.): Pułapki epistemologiczne i metodologiczne w badaniach nad edukacja. Jak sobie z nimi radzić (pp. 212–223). Katowice: UŚ.

Gajdzica, Z. (2019). Zasady organizacji kształcenia w edukacjach inkluzyjnych uczniów z niepełnosprawnością. *Niepełnosprawność. Dyskursy Pedagogiki Specjalnej*, 33, 26–39.

Gajdzica, Z. (2020). Uczeń z lekką niepełnosprawnością intelektualną w szkole ogólnodostępnej. Warszawa: PWN.

Gajdzica, Z., Bełza, M. (Eds.) (2016). Inkluzja edukacyjna. Idee, teorie, koncepcje, modele edukacji włączającej a wybrane aspekty praktyki edukacyjnej. *Problemy Edukacji, Rehabilitacji, Socjalizacji Osób Niepełnosprawnych*, 22.

Gajdzica, Z., Franiok, P. (2013). Special Education of Learners with Mental Retardation in the Czech Republic and Poland. Trans. A. Cienciała. Cieszyn: Stowarzyszenie Wsparcia Społecznego "Feniks."

Garbat, M. (2015). Historia niepełnosprawności. Geneza i rozwój rehabilitacji, pomocy technicznych oraz wsparcia społecznego osób z niepełnosprawnościami. Gdynia: Nove Res.

Grzyb, B. (2013). Uwarunkowania związane z przenoszeniem uczniów niepełnosprawnych ze szkół integracyjnych do specjalnych. Kraków: Impuls.

Gustavsson, A., Zakrzewska-Manterys, E. (Eds.) (1997). Upośledzenie w społecznym zwierciadle. Warszawa: Żak.

Guzik-Tkacz, M., Siegień-Matyjewicz, A. (2015). Leksykon pedagogiki międzykulturowej i etnopedagogiki. Warszawa: Żak.

Hinz, A. (2009). Inklusive Pädagogik in der Schule – veränderter Orientierungsrahmen für die schulische Sonderpädagogik!? Oder doch deren Ende? *Zeitschrift für Heilpädagogik, 5*, 171–179.

Hulek, A. (1992). *Ewolucja integracyjnego systemu kształcenia dziecka niepełnosprawnego.* In: A. Hulek, B. Grochmal-Bach (Eds.), Uczeń niepełnosprawny w szkole masowej (pp. 13–33). Kraków: WSiP.

Jachimczak, B. (2008). *Gotowość nauczycieli szkół ogólnodostępnych do pracy z uczniem o specjalnych potrzebach edukacyjnych.* In: I. Chrzanowska, B. Jachimczak (Eds.), Miejsce Innego we współczesnych naukach o wychowaniu – wyzwania praktyki (pp. 189–200). Łódź: Wydawnictwo Satori.

Kirenko, J. (2007). Indywidualna i społeczna percepcja niepełnosprawności. Lublin: UMCS.

Kirenko, J., Wawer R. (2015). Dystans versus tolerancja. Percepcja niepełnosprawności w badaniach eyetrackingowych. Lublin: UMCS.

Klus-Stańska, D. (2010). Dydaktyka wobec chaosu pojęć i zdarzeń. Warszawa: ŻAK.

Kochanowska, E. (2015). Samoocena nauczycieli w zakresie kompetencji diagnostycznych i pracy z dziećmi ze specjalnymi potrzebami edukacyjnymi na etapie edukacji wczesnoszkolnej. *Niepełnosprawność. Dyskursy Pedagogiki Specjalnej, 20*, 143–153.

Koselleck, R. (2012). Semantyka historyczna. Trans. W. Kunicki. Poznań: Wydawnictwo Poznańskie.

Koselleck, R. (2009). Dzieje pojęć. Studia z semantyki i pragmatyki języka społeczno-politycznego. Trans. J. Marecki, W. Kunicki. Warszawa: Oficyna Naukowa.

Kościelska, M. (1995). Oblicza upośledzenia. Warszawa: PWN.

Kowalik, S. (1989). Upośledzenie umysłowe. Teoria i praktyka rehabilitacji. Warszawa: PWN.

Krause, A. (2000). Integracyjne złudzenie ponowoczesności. Kraków: Impuls.

Krause, A. (2010). Współczesne paradygmaty pedagogiki specjalnej. Kraków: Impuls.

Krause, A. (2004). Człowiek niepełnosprawny wobec przeobrażeń społecznych. Kraków: Impuls.

Kruk-Lasocka, J. (2012). Dostrzec dziecko z perspektywy edukacji włączającej. Wrocław: Wydawnictwo Naukowe Dolnośląskiej Szkoły Wyższej.

Kupisiewicz, Cz., Kupisiewicz, M. (2009). Słownik pedagogiczny. Warszawa: Wydawnictwo Naukowe PWN.

Kupisiewicz, M. (2013). Słowik pedagogiki specjalnej. Warszawa: APS-Wydawnictwo Naukowe PWN.

Kwiatkowska, H. (2008). Pedeutologia. Warszawa: Wydawnictwo Akademickie i Profesjonalne.

Kzanowski, Z. (2011). Przemiany pokoleniowe postaw wobec osób upośledzonych umysłowo. Lublin: UMCS.

Lewowicki, T. (2011). Cztery spojrzenia na wielokulturowość i edukację międzykulturową. *Pogranicze. Studia Społeczne*, 17, 28–38.

Lewowicki, T., Ogrodzka-Mazur, E., Szczurek-Boruta, A. (Eds.) (2000). Edukacja międzykulturowa w Polsce i na świecie. Katowice: UŚ.

Ligus, R. (2012). *Pedagogika inkluzji i zarządzania piętnem – znaczenia, interpretacje, praktyki*. In: P. Rudniki, M. Starnawski, M. Nowak-Dziemianowicz (Eds.), Władza, sens, działanie. Studia wokół związków ideologii i edukacji (pp. 309–330). Wrocław: Wydawnictwo Naukowe Dolnośląskiej Szkoły Wyższej.

Maciarz, A. (2005). Mały leksykon pedagoga specjalnego. Kraków: Impuls.

Męczkowska, A. (2003). *Kompetencja*. In: T. Pilch (Ed.), Encyklopedia pedagogiczna XXI wieku (pp. 692–696). Warszawa: Żak, Vol. II. G–Ł.

Milerski, B., Śliwerski, B. (Eds.) (2000). Pedagogika. Leksykon. Warszawa: Wydawnictwo Naukowe PWN.

Minczakiewicz, E. (1996). *Postawy nauczycieli i uczniów szkół powszechnych wobec dzieci niepełnosprawnych*. In: W. Dykcik (Ed.), Społeczeństwo wobec autonomii osób niepełnosprawnych (pp. 131–144). Poznań: Wydawnictwo Eruditus.

Nikitorowicz, J. (2017). Etnopedagogika w kontekście wielokulturowości i ustawicznie kształtującej się tożsamości. Kraków: Impuls.

Okoń, W. (1995). Wprowadzenie do dydaktyki ogólnej. Warszawa: Żak.

Okoń, W. (2004). Nowy słownik pedagogiczny. Warszawa: Żak.

Olszewski, S., Parys, K. (2016). Rozumieć chaos. Rzecz o terminach i znaczeniach im nadawanych w pedagogice specjalnej. Kraków: Wydawnictwo Naukowe Uniwersytetu Pedagogicznego.

Ostrowska, A. (1997). *Postawy społeczeństwa polskiego w stosunku do osób niepełnosprawnych*. In: A. Gustavsson, E. Zakrzewska-Manterys (Eds.), Upośledzenie w społecznym zwierciadle (pp. 75–95). Warszawa: Żak.

Oświata i wychowanie w roku szkolnym 2016 / 17. Główny Urząd statystyczny. Warszawa 2017.

Parys, K. (2014). Zjawisko pozoru w systemie kształcenia uczniów niepełnosprawnych – próba identyfikacji i propozycje rozwiązań. *Interdyscyplinarne Konteksty Pedagogiki Specjalnej, 4, 29–55.*

Pielecki, A. (2013). Zmiany postaw młodzieży wobec osób niepełnosprawnych. Lublin: UMCS.

Pielecki, A., Kazanowski, Z. (2001). *Przygotowanie nauczycieli do realizacji założeń integracji szkolnej dzieci niepełnosprawnych,* In: Z. Palak (Ed.), Pedagogika specjalna w reformowanym ustroju edukacyjnym (pp. 207–214). Lublin: UMCS.

Pilecka, W., Pilecki, J. (2002). *Poland.* In: H. Mazurek, M. A. Wizner (Eds.), Comparative Studies in Special Education (pp. 334–350). Washington: Gallaudet University Press.

Półturzycki, J. (1997). Dydaktyka dla nauczycieli. Toruń: UMK.

Průcha, J., Walterovà, E., Mareš, J. (2003). Pedagogický slovnik. Praha: Portàl.

Rieser, R. (2013). *The Struggle for Inclusion: The Growth of a Movement.* In: L. Barton (Ed.), Disability Politics & The Struggle for Change (pp. 132–148). London and New York: Routledge Taylor & Francis Group.

Rozporządzenie MEN z dnia 17 listopada 2010r. Dziennik Ustaw nr 228 [Directive of the Ministry of National Education of 17th November, 2010. Journal of Laws No 228].

Rozporządzenie MEN z dnia 24 lipca 2015 w sprawie warunków organizowania kształcenia, wychowania i opieki dla dzieci i młodzieży niepełnosprawnych, niedostosowanych społecznie i zagrożonych niedostosowaniem społecznym. Dziennik Ustaw z dnia 7 sierpnia 2015, poz. 1113 [Directive of the Ministry of National Education of July 24, 2014 on the conditions of organizing education and care for disabled, socially maladjusted and endangered with social maladjustment children and youth. Journal of Laws, 7th August 2015, p. 1113].

Rozporządzenie Ministra Edukacji Narodowej z dnia 18 września 2008 r. w sprawie orzeczeń i opinii wydawanych przez zespoły orzekające działające w publicznych poradniach psychologiczno-pedagogicznych. Dziennik Ustaw nr 173, poz. 1072 [Directive of the Ministry of National Education of September 18, 2008 on certificates and opinions issued by certification panels at public psychological-pedagogical counselling centres. Journal of Laws No 173, p. 1072].

Rozporządzenie Ministra Edukacji Narodowej z dnia 20 marca 2018 r. w sprawie wysokości wskaźników zwiększających kwoty dotacji celowej na wyposażenie szkół podstawowych w podręczniki, materiały edukacyjne i materiały ćwiczeniowe dla uczniów niepełnosprawnych. Dziennik Ustaw z 2018 r. poz. 611 [Directive of the Ministry of National Education of March, 20 2018 on the value of indicators increasing the subvention aimed at equipping primary schools with coursebooks, educational and exercise materials for disabled learners. Journal of Laws, 2018 p. 611].

Rozporządzenie Ministra Edukacji Narodowej z dnia 30 kwietnia 2013 r. w sprawie zasad udzielania i organizacji pomocy psychologiczno-pedagogicznej w publicznych przedszkolach, szkołach i placówkach.

64   Inclusive education of learners with disability in Poland

Dziennik Ustaw z dnia 7 maja 2013, poz. 532 [Directive of the Ministry of National Education of April 30, 2018 on the principles of providing and organizing psychological-pedagogical support in public kindergartens, schools and centres. Journal of Laws, 7th May 2013, p. 532].

Sękowski, A., Zieliński, J. (2010). *Psychospołeczne uwarunkowania zmian postaw wobec osób z niepełnosprawnością.* In: Z. Palak, A. Bujnowska, A. Pawlak (Eds.), Edukacyjne i rehabilitacyjne konteksty rozwoju osób z niepełnosprawnością w różnych okresach życia (pp. 13–27). Lublin: UMCS.

Skibska, J. (2016). Edukacja włączająca w opinii nauczycieli edukacji wczesnoszkolnej – analiza segmentacyjna. Doniesienie z badań. *Problemy Edukacji, Rehabilitacji, Socjalizacji Osób Niepełnosprawnych*, 22, 161–174.

Speck, O. (2013). Inkluzja edukacyjna a pedagogika lecznicza. Trans. A. Grysińska. Gdańsk: Harmonia Universalis.

System Informacji Oświatowej [System of Educational Information]. www.niepelnosprawni.gov.pl/p,123,edukacja (access: May 2018).

Szewczuk, W. (1993). *Zasady nauczania – uczenia się i wychowania.* In: W. Pomykało (Ed.), Encyklopedia Pedagogiczna (pp. 978–989). Warszawa: Innowacja.

Szkudlarek, T. (2003). *Pedagogika międzykulturowa.* In: Z. Kwieciński, B. Śliwerski (Eds.), Pedagogika, Vol. 1 (pp. 415–424). Warszawa: Wydawnictwo Naukowe PWN.

Szumski, G. (2006). Integracyjne kształcenie niepełnosprawnych. Warszawa: Wydawnictwo Naukowe PWN.

Szumski, G. (2010). Wokół edukacji włączającej. Efekty kształcenia uczniów z niepełnosprawnością intelektualną w stopniu lekkim w klasach specjalnych, integracyjnych i ogólnodostępnych. Warszawa: Wydawnictwo APS.

Thomas, G., Loxley, A. (2007). Deconstructing Special Education and Constructing Inclusion. New York: Open University Press.

Tuohy, D. (2002). Dusza szkoły. O tym, co sprzyja zmianie i rozwojowi. Trans. K. Kruszewski. Warszawa: Wydawnictwo Naukowe PWN.

Ustawa o systemie oświaty z 7 września 1991r. Dziennik Ustaw nr 67 z 1996 r. poz. 329 [Act on the educational system of 7th September 1991. Journal of Laws No 67, 1996, p. 329].

Waszkiewicz, A., Dumnicka, K. (2012). *Finansowanie uczniów z niepełnosprawnościami*. In: Równe szanse w dostępie do edukacji osób z niepełnosprawnościami. Analiza i zalecenia. Warszawa: Rzecznik Praw Obywatelskich.

Wyczesany, J. (2005). Pedagogika upośledzonych umysłowo. Kraków: Impuls.

Zacharuk, T. (2008). Wprowadzenie do edukacji inkluzyjnej. Siedlce: Wydawnictwo Akademii Podlaskiej.

Załącznik do Rozporządzenia MEN z dnia 18 grudnia 2013 r. w sprawie sposobu podziału części oświatowej subwencji ogólnej dla jednostek samorządu terytorialnego w roku 2014, Dziennik Ustaw z 2013 r., poz. 1687 [Annex to the Directive of the Ministry of National Education of 18th December 2013 on the way of distributing the educational part of general subvention for territorial government units in 2014, Journal of Laws, 2013, p. 1687].

Zamkowska, A. (2000). Wybrane problemy integracyjnego kształcenia. Radom: Wydawnictwo Politechniki Radomskiej.

Zamkowska, A. (2009). Wsparcie edukacyjne uczniów z upośledzeniem umysłowym w stopniu lekkim w różnych formach kształcenia na I etapie edukacji. Radom: Wydawnictwo PR.

Zarządzenie nr 29 Ministra Edukacji Narodowej z dnia 4 października 1993 r. w sprawie zasad organizowania opieki nad uczniami niepełnosprawnymi, ich kształcenia w ogólnodostępnych i integracyjnych publicznych przedszkolach, szkołach i placówkach oraz organizacji kształcenia specjalnego. Dziennik Urzędowy MEN z dnia 15 listopada 1993 r. [Directive of the Ministry of National Education of 4th October 1993. on the principles of organizing care for disabled learners, their education in mainstream and integrated public kindergartens, schools and institutions and on the organization of special education. Official Journal of the Ministry of National Education of 15th November 1993].

Robin McWilliam

Chapter 2 Inclusive education of learners with disability in the United States of America

Introduction

Competing Values

Inclusion is but one value in American society, including education. In this chapter, I will discuss how people have taken this value to shape policies and practices – sometimes successfully, sometimes not. The value of placing and keeping children with disabilities in the same contexts as their peers without disabilities is well-known in the U.S. Yet, it is not the only value guiding our ideas about how schools and communities should be run.

Another strong American value is specialization – the notion that people should be narrowly trained to a high level, so they can diagnose problems specifically and accurately and can make recommendations or formal treatment plans. If there is a water leak in our kitchen ceiling, one do not want simply a general contractor, but a certified roof repair expert. Similarly, in medical care, the primary care physician is often the gatekeeper for specialists. Americans place much stock in expert knowledge and skill. This confidence in specialists might even cross over to reliance on specialists. When families of children with disabilities put their confidence in specialists, rather than generalists, the pernicious slide towards overspecialization begins. Everybody wants a piece of the child (McWilliam, 2011). Therefore, inclusion and specialization might be competing forces.

Another value in special education and other services to children with disabilities in the U.S. is family-centred care. The main educational law mandating education in the least restrictive environment (Individuals with Disabilities Education Improvement Act, IDEA) has numerous safeguards for the rights of families of children with disabilities. However, the value of families is quite fractured, with highly family-centred practices involved in some early intervention programs for infants and toddlers but with a dis-regard for families, other than their due-process rights. For example, fam-ilies' needs for support around their child's functioning in home routines are typically not addressed on individualized education programs, nor are family needs. It is as if the education establishment acts as though the children are helicoptered in from the orphanage. Nevertheless, by law and some people's morality, families are honoured, which can bump up against values of specialization and inclusion.

Guralnick and Bruder (2016) identified four key goals to inclusion in early childhood. First, children and families had to have access to inclusive programs. As discussed later in this chapter, 40 % of children 3 years of age were spending 10 hours a week or more in specialized settings rather than in regular early childhood programs (U.S. Department of Education – Office of Special Education and Rehabilitative Services – Office of Special Education Programs, 2017). Second, curricula and routines have not gen-erally accommodated children with disabilities, largely owing to the lack of preparation of the teaching staff to do this (Guralnick et al., 2016). Third, children with developmental disabilities make progress in inclusive settings, and children without disabilities do not suffer (Odom, Buysse, Soukakou, 2011). Fourth, interactions and friendships can be fostered in an inclusive setting (Buysse, 1993). Therefore, the current status in the U.S. is mixed: The country is probably at the vanguard in some ways but needs to improve or at least obtain more data.

American societal values of self-determination and independence

From its founding, the U.S. has put much value in the independence of the individual. The Declaration of Independence is the document the Founding Fathers drew up to establish their autonomy from Great Britain. Although framed for the 13 original colonies, its message is mirrored in, for example, the constitution of the United States and its amendments, such as the right to bear arms, the right of free speech, the right to due pro-cess, and so on. We might assume that a culture placing so much value on autonomy would place low value on relatedness – of wanting to connect with others, especially people who are different. Some social psychologists have, however, questioned the notion that autonomy and relatedness are mutually exclusive (Chirkov, Ryan, Kim, Kaplan, 2003). What motivates people to act independently? In self-determination theory, psychologists make a distinction between autonomous motivation and controlled motivation, with the former meaning the individual acts with a sense of volition and the latter meaning the individual acts under pressure – having to do something (Gagné, Deci, 2005). When a person with disabilities can function independently, more or less when and how he or she wants to, it is an expression of self-determination.

The U.S. embraces a can-do culture, favouring independence over interdependence. One societal value, for example, is the cowboy mentality, with the Marlboro Man as the icon. The Marlboro Man was a ruggedly handsome, hypermasculine cowboy featured in advertisements for Marlboro cigarettes. When George W. Bush used tough talk about dealing with terrorists, after the World Trade Center and Pentagon bombings, he played up his cowboy side – the one aligned with his riding horses on a ranch in Texas, as opposed to his upper class background from Kennebunkport, Maine, and his attending Yale Law School. Ronald Reagan, the actor, liked to be photographed on a horse on his Californian ranch. Cowboy movies from the U.S., known as "westerns," were a major film genre. Perhaps the most independent-acting, strong-featured president of the U.S. was Theodore Roosevelt, whose belief in rugged individualism set the tone for many politicians to follow.

A second societal value is the business ethic, captured in the country's right-wing leaning politics, commitment to capitalism, and development of big businesses. In a text book about American culture for English-language learners, three pairs of American values are discussed (Datesman, Crandall, Kearny, 1997). Each pair has one advantage and one price to pay for that advantage. For the benefit of the value of individual freedom is the price of self-reliance. For the benefit of the value of equality of opportunity, the price is competition. For the benefit of the value of the American dream ("the opportunity for a better life and a higher standard of living"), the price is hard work. Now, all these so-called prices are prices many Americans are happy to pay. Self-reliance, competition, and hard work are the legs of the American stool of business.

One hears calls for running universities, schools, and government agencies on a so-called business model. This assumes those entities will be less wasteful – more efficient. Especially in the current presidential administration, the U.S. has apparently eschewed notions of interdependence. For children with disabilities, however, interdependence might be a strange but necessary corollary of independence. Ironically, they might need others to be able to exercise their independence.

American cultural values of equity and fairness

Reject monarchy

Although far from perfect is its execution, the U.S. has a cultural tradition of promoting equity and fairness. For example, the country broke away from the aristocratic structures of Great Britain, with its nobility and other forms of aristocracy. I believe the U.S. has replaced these structures, however, with a high value on material possessions and income.

Home for religious tolerance

The U.S. likes to think of itself as a bastion of religious tolerance. In fact, many of the first settlers came to the American colonies to escape religious persecution in England. Pilgrims and Puritans came to their shining "city upon a hill," as Governor John Winthrop called it. Freedom of religion is one of the protections under the U.S. constitution. Despite this welcoming stance towards religion, Protestant Christianity is the de facto religion of the country, as seen in the motto "In God we trust," in the use of usually Christian but sometimes nondenominational prayers, and in the observance of Christian national holidays (e.g., Easter, Christmas). Compared to many other countries, however, the U.S. is largely accepting of many religions.

ADA and IDEA

Along with its republican (nonmonarchist) ethos and its religious tolerance, another American value regarding equity and fairness has resulted in legislation protecting the rights of children and adults with disabilities. Despite the U.S.'s shameful failure to ratify the United Nations Convention on the Rights of Persons with Disabilities, it has arguably led the way, internationally, in legislation. The Americans with Disabilities Act was the model for the Convention on the Rights of Persons with Disabilities. This law forces businesses, public agencies, and communities to ensure people with disabilities have access to the same opportunities people without disabilities do. This includes physical access and social access such as employment. The Individuals with Disabilities Education Act is the legislation that ensures that children birth through 21 have access to education through appropriate assessment, services, and settings.

Professionals building inclusive practices have benefitted from American societal mores around equal opportunity and due process, which is the constitutional right to fairness in the legal system. Striving for an egalitarian society, tolerance for people who are different, and supporting legislation have formed the American idea about inclusion.

2.1. Theoretical foundations of inclusive education

To understand inclusion in the U.S., it is necessary to examine the history of the education of learners with disabilities, the types of inclusive practices used in the U.S., and the ties between the cultural determinants mentioned in the section Cultural determinants of inclusive education (How has culture influenced the development and condition of inclusive education?) and current practices.

2.1.1. Historical outline of education for disabled learners in the USA

In the U.S., we can think of three stages of inclusion because the terminology was different for each stage: (1) In the 1960s to the early 1980s, it was mainstreaming; (2) in the 1980s, it was integration and the regular education initiative; and (3) from the late 1980s until the present, it has been inclusion. Using the framework of a publication on Reflections on Inclusion (McLeskey, 2007), 10 issues formed the vertebrae of inclusion:

The early history

The seminal and often cited article by Dunn (1968), "Special education for the mildly retarded – Is much of it justifiable?" revolutionized special educators' thinking about how and where teachers should teach children with disabilities or at risk for disabilities. He objected to general educators sending children who were difficult to teach to special education, resulting in an over-identification of children from minority backgrounds as having mild intellectual disabilities ("mental retardation," in the terminology of that time). In these early years, special education was reconceptualised as a continuum or cascade of services (Deno, 1970). This cascade consisted of seven levels, from children in regular classes (Level I), to full-time special classes (Level IV), to homebound (Level VI), to instruction in hospital settings (Level VII).

Building support for inclusion

Once policy makers introduced mainstreaming, yet before inclusion was the rallying point, experts called for a merger of regular and special education (McLeskey, 2007). The 1980s were a ripe decade for fostering ideas that, to this day, systems have not put in place but that still seem relevant. All of education was under scrutiny, especially when the report A Nation at Risk (National Commission on Excellence in Education, 1983) characterized American education as mediocre. Madeleine Will (1986), an official in the U.S. Department of Education, advocated that general and special educators share the responsibility for children with disabilities. She alerted the field(s) that a central problem was the common idea that children with disabilities should be pulled out from classrooms and educated in resource rooms (McWilliam, 1996).

At this time, the terminology for what is now called inclusion was changing. The progression has been mainstreaming, integration, the Regular Education Initiative, and inclusion. Regardless of the terms, which generally have pushed for more "full inclusion," even the current term "inclusion" is rife with misunderstanding (McLeskey, 2007). The Regular Education Initiative (REI) was aimed primarily at children with mild disabilities (Reynolds, Wang, Walberg, 1987) and called for a merger of general and special education and for no categorization within disabilities. These experts presented research showing the same instructional strategies worked across disability groups. Other experts expanded these ideas to argue that children with severe disabilities also should be educated alongside children without disabilities (Stainback, Stainback, 1984), again with the argument that techniques from special education could work with all students – what later became a foundation of universal design for learning

(UDL). The major theme in the 1980s, therefore, was a demand to merge general and special education.

Reservations about inclusion

In the 1990s, some researchers cautioned the field about such a radical move. Advocates for students with disabilities, in particular those with severe disabilities, took a drastic stance focused on no special education, criticism of the standard curriculum, and the needs of students with severe disabilities, almost to the point of ignoring students with milder disabilities (Fuchs, Fuchs, 1994). Kauffman (1993), in a complete departure from the REI advocates argued that instruction should be disaggregated for different types of students, that the foundations of special education should be re-examined, and that the empirical base of special education should be strengthened.

Research related to inclusion and program effectiveness

"Special classes were found to be significantly inferior to regular class placement for students with below average IQs, significantly superior to regular classes for behavioural disordered, emotionally disturbed, and learning-disabled children" (Carlberg, Kavale, 1980, p. 295). Much of the research has been contradictory. Carlberg and Kavale conducted one of the first meta-analyses in special education, incorporating 50 studies. Researchers did find successes for both children with mild disabilities and those with severe disabilities (Salend, Duhaney, 2007). Some studies showed negative effects for inclusion with youth in secondary programs, they preferred inclusive settings because that was where their friends were.

Teacher attitudes towards inclusion

General-education teachers now had children with disabilities in their classrooms. How did they feel about this? Presumably, their attitudes towards mainstreaming/inclusion would affect their teaching and caring. Scruggs and Mastropieri (1996) synthesized the research on teacher perceptions of mainstreaming/inclusion from 1958 to 1995. They counted the number of respondents in the studies who agreed with statements related to (a) support for mainstreaming/inclusion, (b) willingness to mainstream students with disabilities, (c) and the effects of mainstreaming/inclusion. Approximately two thirds of the teachers were in favour of mainstreaming/inclusion, but only one third felt they had the training or resources to meet the needs of these students. General-education teachers' concerns with inclusion were mostly about procedural issues – how was this thing called inclusion going to work (Waldron, 2007)? Waldron wrote: "Teachers are cautious about change until they are sure that the change is appropriate and manageable" (p. 185). The participants in the studies Scruggs and Mastropieri reviewed varied experiences with inclusion, so the attitudes might have been confounded by experience. In a study of perspectives of teachers who were all in well-designed inclusive programs and teachers on a waiting list for such programs, only 10 % of the teachers in inclusive programs and 20 % on the waiting list did not support inclusion (McLeskey, Waldron, So, Swanson, Loveland, 2001).

The adolescence of inclusive practices

In the U.S., by law, schools must incorporate response to intervention (RTI), which now tends to be known as multi-tiered systems of support (MTSS), which are described later. Experts proposed a service delivery approach called collaborative consultation as a way of assisting students before referring them for a formal evaluation for special education (Bauwens, Hourcade, Friend, 1989). This approach involved teamwork and left the responsibility for instruction with the general educator (Idol, Nevin, Paolucci-Whitcomb, 1994). Another approach towards teamwork was cooperative teaching, where the general-education and the special-education teachers taught in the room together. Yet another approach described in the 1980s and 1990s was teacher assistance teams (Chalfant, Van Dusen Pysh, 1989): "The teacher assistance team (TAT) is a school-based problem-solving unit used to assist teachers in generating intervention strategies" (p. 50). Whereas traditional teams in schools were child oriented, TATs were teacher oriented.

When Idol et al. (1994) described collaborative consultation, it provoked discussion about the extent to which it was collaborative versus expert in perspective (Epanchin, Friend, 2007). Epanchin and Friend considered collaborative consultation to be an "expert-based model" (p. 213), when, in fact, experts have described it as the opposite of expert based (Woods, Wilcox, Friedman, Murch, 2011). They did emphasize that collaboration required trust and respect. Professionals were not, however, always receptive to preservice or inservice preparation because of the "dismissive belief that educators already know 'how to talk to each other'" (Epanchin, Friend, p. 216). In these times, therefore, experts sought to define collaboration between general and special educators.

Curriculum-based measurement

In the mid-1980s, professionals were concerned about the commercial, norm-referenced evaluation instruments being used to classify students with disabilities, to program for them, and to monitor their progress (Deno, 1985). The proposed alternative, curriculum-based measurement (CBM) standardized observations of performance in the curriculum and was used for the gamut of assessment purposes: screening, referral, IEP planning, student progress, and program evaluation. CBM was proposed as a means to improve communication for educational decision making, increase sensitivity to changes in student performance, improve the data base about student growth, refer to peers' performance on the same measure, and contain costs.

Classroom instruction in inclusive settings

By the late 1980s, students with disabilities, particularly mild ones such as learning disabilities, were being placed in general-education classrooms. Teachers' and researchers' attention turned to what methods should be used with these children in these settings. Did classroom teachers have the requisite expertise? Would children without disabilities ridicule those with? What were the respective roles of the general and special education teachers? (Haager, 2007). One innovation proposed was classwide peer tutoring, in which pairs of students tutor each other and earn points for correct responding and for tutoring (Delquadri, Greenwood, Whorton, Carta, Hall, 1986). Teachers wanted to make adaptations for the mainstreamed students, but found the adaptations less feasible than desirable (Schumm, Vaughn, 1991). In this study of 93 teachers, the most feasible of the listed adaptations were (a) providing reinforcement and encouragement and (b) establishing a routine appropriate for the mainstreamed student. The least feasible were using computers and using alternative materials.

Inclusion in secondary schools

Questions were raised about the purpose of inclusion in secondary schools, such as whether students with disabilities should have the same curriculum as students without disabilities, whether their curriculum should be academic or vocational, whether inclusion was a matter of equality, and whether inclusive education would promote transition to employment and independent living (Kochhar-Bryant, 2007). Gene Edgar bemoaned the poor employment outcomes and the extent of dropping out by students with mild intellectual disabilities and he recommended a move away from academic towards vocational programs (Edgar, 1987). He acknowledged that this move would cause the untenable tracking – a track on to which already devalued students (poor, minority, stressful families) would be shunted. His position was not that such a track should be built, but that that should not stop educators from facing the fact that inclusive settings were producing poor employment and independent-living outcomes for students with mild disabilities.

Inclusive education and students with severe disabilities

Beginning in 1970, the cascade system of special education services held sway over special education placement decisions for many years (Deno, 1970). This system contained a number of settings differing by how restrictive they were. The American special education law has always mandated that students should be placed in the least restrictive environment that allows them to learn. Educators assumed that the more severe the student's disabilities, especially severe intellectual disabilities, the more restrictive the appropriate setting would be. Education and care of people of all ages with disabilities were influenced by principles of normalization (Wolfensberger, 1970), which rested on the belief that people with intellectual disabilities should be able to engage in culturally normative behaviour and that the means to that end should be culturally normative. Wolfensberger (1983) later renamed normalization social role valorization because (a) many people used the term normalization in widely varying and informal ways and (b) the principle had become "clarified to be the establishment, enhancement, or defence of the social role(s) of a person or group" (p. 234). At the end of the 1970s, educators turned their attention to the questionable methods of paying more attention to a student's mental age than chronological age. Experts developed curricula consisting of functional, chronological-age-appropriate skills to be taught in natural environments (Brown et al., 1979). This strategy was developed to teach adolescents and young adult students.

What did general-education teachers think about having students with severe disabilities in their classroom? In a mixed-method study of 19 teachers, 17 of them had a "transformational" experience, moving from negative to more positive reactions (Giangreco, Dennis, Cloninger, Edelman, Schattman, 1993). The teachers found the various professionals who visited the classroom to vary in their helpfulness. They identified the kind of help they could do without: separate goals by specialists, disruption to the classroom routine, and overspecialization (e.g., abnormalizing equipment, use of incomprehensible jargon, strategies that could not be implemented in regular routines).

2.1.2. Major approaches to inclusive education

Social-inclusion theory involves asking who is to be included and how much a person is included (Gidley, Hampson, Wheeler, Bereded-Samuel, 2010). This perspective was an Australasian one, derived from a British policy. Notably, the demographic differentiation of social groupings did not include disability even though it did include socio-economic status, culture, religion, and so on. The theoretical background to inclusive education must be related to a theory regarding the following tenets:

- Students should have access to all the resources the school provides to students in general;
- Students should feel as though they belong to a classroom and a school (i.e., membership);
- Students should have access to appropriate education in their neighbourhood school;

- Students should have social opportunities to interact with all kinds of students at the school;
- Students should be engaged in academic, social, and vocational activities in the school;
- Students should be as independent as they can be in school.

Unfortunately, no theory adequately captures these six tenets. Gidley et al. (2010) have described a nested schema of inclusion, with social inclusion interpreted narrowly as access, more broadly as participation, and most broadly as empowerment. In education, these interpretations work – to an extent. The philosophy (as opposed to theory) of inclusion implies that inclusion is good. Who would want to exclude someone from an activity everyone else gets to have? Yet, what about voluntary social exclusion or, in our field, educational segregation (Barry, 1998)? Voluntary social isolation occurs when a person or community (e.g., religious organization) chooses to separate from others. Social exclusion, however, occurs when the person has no choice; others have kept him or her out.

In English-speaking countries, three major approaches to inclusive education have been the psycho-medical legacy, reverse mainstreaming, and full inclusion with natural proportions. It is well known that a traditional view on education of children with disabilities was grounded in a medical model, in which the deficit in the child was the object of focus. This within-child view, also adopted by psychologists in the 1960s and 1970s, gradually evolved to an understanding that instruction and other environmental factors played a more important role in making decisions about educational placement and instruction (Clough, Corbett, 2000).

By the 1970s, when the Education of All Handicapped Children Act was passed and even to this day, inclusion per se is not mandated. Instead, children are required to be educated in the least restrictive environment. This opens the door to interpretation and legal wrangling. Ironically, the American law is credited as being one of the most progressive for promoting inclusion, yet the term is absent from the law.

Used more in early childhood special education than in school-aged education, reverse mainstreaming has been one way educators have edged their way towards more inclusive education (Rafferty, Boettcher, Griffin, 2001). Sometimes called integrated education, reverse mainstreaming involves enrolling children without disabilities in programs created for children with disabilities.

The most radical call for inclusive education has been for full inclusion with natural proportions (MacMillan, Gresham, Forness, 1996). This concept involves the placement of children in classrooms designed for all children (especially those without disabilities), with no greater proportion of those with disabilities than found in the community population. Experts soon considered such a far-reaching concept illusory in terms of meeting the educational needs of children with disabilities (Kauffman, Hallahan, 1995). Doug and Lynn Fuchs (Fuchs, Fuchs, 2012) provide a nuanced distinction between inclusionists, who advocate for a cascade of services, and full inclusionists, who advocate for all children to be in regular classrooms. One of their most compelling arguments in favour of the inclusionist position is that classrooms have limits on the extent to which they can change to meet the needs of all children with disabilities. They do recognize, however, that, countering that argument, most teachers do not differentiate their teaching to the spectrum of children in their classrooms.

Most school districts in the U.S. offer a continuum of services from self-contained schools, through self-contained classrooms, through resource rooms, to full-time inclusion. The American law allows for parents and schools to determine what the least restrictive environment is, for the child to gain access to the curriculum, to achieve learning outcomes, and to participate socially with other children. Unfortunately, determining this environment often requires mediation or court action.

2.1.3. Cultural determinants of inclusive education

The American culture has influenced the development of inclusive education through parallels with civil rights, beliefs in non-discrimination, and the honouring of diversity. One of the most significant aspects of the relatively short U.S. history is its reconciliation of a history of slavery and racism. The country has gone through struggles for civil rights for women, for people from minority races and ethnicities, for gay people, and others. People with disabilities have similarly been seen as an oppressed group whose rights need protecting. They were no longer to be disenfranchised, so laws such as IDEA and the Americans with Disabilities Act were designed to ensure they were not discriminated against. Families were encouraged and educated to advocate for their children. Today, self-determination, in which people with disabilities are given opportunities to make decisions for themselves, is a well-accepted part of the disability experience. This begins in adolescence, when youth participate in their IEP and transition-planning processes.

The cultural concept of non-discrimination has its place in inclusive education. In the IEP process, children are protected from discrimination in terms of their placement – where they receive their education. If a family believes the child has been placed in an inappropriate setting, they can pursue "due process" and legal action, protected under IDEA. Special education researchers have noted that a disproportional number of minority (especially Black and Latino) children are in special education (Sullivan, Bal, 2013). A major concern has been that teachers wanted these children removed from their classrooms, which shows that special education was seen as something outside the regular classroom, not an inclusive practice. Another concern was that behaviours of white and Asian children were interpreted differently from the same behaviours of African American and Latino children, which would constitute discrimination on the basis of race or ethnicity. Attention to disproportionality in special education has increased some educators' sensitivity to this potential institutionalized (i.e., largely unrecognized) discrimination. Special education was seen as a bad thing because it was excluding the children sent to it. Paradoxically, education officials have striven to increase the percentage of children referred to early intervention, through "child find" efforts, as specified in IDEA. Early intervention is considered a good thing. I speculate that one reason for this paradox is that participation in early intervention does not imply removal from natural environments. Of course, participation in special education should not imply this removal either.

The United States culture honours diversity, even though pockets of ethnocentricity are aplenty. People with disabilities have an identity and are included in efforts to promote and celebrate diversity. It might be true that those children with visible disabilities might have an easier path than those with invisible disabilities other than their behaviour. That is, a child in a wheelchair or using a cane is generally treated with kindness at school, but a child with unpredictable or unusual behaviour, perhaps as a consequence of intellectual disability, autism spectrum disorder, or attention deficit hyperactive disorder, might not be treated with kindness. In general, American society honours diversity, advocates for non-discrimination, and has a history of civil rights for disenfranchised people, all of which have influenced inclusive education.

2.2. Inclusive education in practice

2.2.1. Organization of inclusive education

Inclusive education in the United States is organized through a cascade of services, and data are reported to Congress (the Senate and House of Representatives). The system is essentially one of two buckets, as I explain below.

As mentioned earlier, special education has been organized in the U.S. as a cascade of services, the critical components of which are specialized instruction to students, collaboration between special-education personnel and general educators, organizational supports from the administration, and benefits for typically developing students (Odom et al., 2011). The main options in this cascade have been the following:

1. Regular classroom(s) all day;
2. Some resource room (i.e., pull out);
3. Integrated or itinerant;
4. Much resource room;
5. Token inclusion;
6. Separate class;
7. Separate school.

The Office of Special Education Programs in the U.S. Department of Education produces a report to congress each year. Generally, the reports provide data from a couple of years before the report is actually made. The latest available report is the 2017 one, which reports on data from the school year 2014–15 (U.S. Department of Education – Office of Special Education and Rehabilitative Services – Office of Special Education Programs, 2017). The Report to Congress includes the percentage of infants and toddlers birth through age 2 served under IDEA by primary early intervention setting. In 2015, the latest year for which data are available, 88.7 % were served in the home, 7.3 % were served in community-based settings (e.g., child care programs), and 4 % were served in other settings. These are known as the natural-environments data. It should be remembered that this was for the primary early intervention setting. In some states, children could receive their "special instruction" (a generalist approach) as their primary early intervention but could receive speech, occupational, or physical therapy in clinics, offices, or hospitals. Therefore, these percentages do not reflect all early intervention visits – only those of the primary service. For the same year, the percentage of children ages 3 through 5, by educational environment, was as follows:

Regular early childhood program:

At least 10 hours per week and majority	39.4
At least 10 hours per week, majority elsewhere	16.9
Less than 10 hours per week and majority	5.4
Less than 10 hours per week, majority elsewhere	4.9
Separate class	22.7
Separate school	2.5
Residential facility	0
Home	2.0
Service provider location	6.2

The classification of educational environments for students ages 6 through 21 is different. These are known as the least restrictive environment (LRE) data. Here are the percentages:

Inside the regular class:

80 % or more of the day	62.7
40 % to 79 % of the day	18.7
Less than 40 % of the day	13.5
Separate school	2.8
Residential facility	0.3
Homebound/hospital	0.4
Correctional facility	0.2
Partially placed in private school	1.5

The data from the states and territories vary considerably. For example, 83.6 % of Alabama students are served in the regular class for 80 % or more of the day, whereas in New Jersey only 46.0 % of the students are served in this environment.

Environments to some extent reveal the organization of inclusive education, but the decision point about placement, also known as setting or environment, occurs technically during the IFSP or IEP meeting. The order of decisions is supposed to be the following:

1. Determine eligibility;
2. Determine needs;
3. Determine outcomes or goals;
4. Determine services and placement.

The extent of inclusion, therefore, should be decided on the basis of the least restrictive environment in which the student can receive the services to meet his or her goals. This order is important, because the goals should be for the child to be able to learn and to participate in the regular curriculum, according to the law. Unfortunately, the law does not truly address functioning at home, school, and community in the way the International Classification of Functioning, Disability and Health recommends (World Health Organization, 2007). At the IEP meeting are the child (if appropriate), the family, a teacher, therapists (optionally), and a school district administrator. When placement and service decisions are made, ideally, the process is collaborative, with the child and family having a significant role (Zhang, Bennett, 2003). In too many meetings, however, the school personnel inform the family of the suitable placement they have available for their child, and the family assumes they must accept it (Wagner, Newman, Cameto, Javitz, Valdes, 2012).

IEP meetings are for children with disabilities only. Therefore, there is a two-bucket system: children are either in the disability bucket or not. IDEA attempted to create more of a continuum with a multi-tiered systems of support (Jimerson, Burns, VanDerHeyden, 2015). Also known as response to intervention (Fletcher, Vaughn, 2009), the system is supposed to operate like a pyramid:

In Tier 1, the regular classroom, teachers should be differentiating their instruction for all children, regardless of which of the two buckets they fall into. If this differentiated instruction does not work, they can refer the child for Tier 2, which is typically where special education enters. Some versions of Tier 2 are focused on small-group supports, such as tracked reading programs. In these programs, children of different reading skill levels are in different groups. Some versions are focused on individualized supports, usually requiring referral to special education, which starts a whole bureaucratic and legal process (see the order of decisions above). If the child does not respond well to individualized or group supports, he or she is referred for Tier 3 supports. These supports usually require a structured, detailed assessment of the learning or behaviour problem and a detailed procedure for teaching the child. The procedure is most often a behaviour intervention plan with a set procedure, with established antecedents and consequences, a data collection system, and decision rules based on the data. The concept behind multi-tiered systems of support is that a child moves to a more restrictive or structured level of support to the extent that he or she does not respond to the lower tier. One can immediately see that this puts a large onus on the regular teacher to provide as much universal support to as many children as possible. Questions still remain about whether a child can come back down through the tiers, once referred up the tiers, and can a child remain in Tier 1 for some things and in Tier 2 for selected other things.

2.2.2. Financing inclusive education

Financing inclusive education in the United States comes from the federal government, pursuant to two laws, from state government and from local government. First, three parts of IDEA provide funding that has an impact on inclusive education. Part C of the law provides funding to states to run infant-toddler programs. These funds are used to finance the Part C office, including a coordinator for personnel development and a child find (i.e., securing referrals) program. They also often include funding for state-wide service coordination (like case management). Occasionally, they fund direct services, when other sources of payment do not. In infant-toddler services, insurance – both public and private – often plays a considerable role. Public insurance is called Medicaid, although some states use their own name for this funding. Private insurance is for health care, which often includes the therapies and case management and sometimes also special instruction (i.e., generalist early intervention). Each state chooses the lead agency for administering early intervention. This can be, for example, the state education department, the state health department, the governor's office, or a children's bureau. This means that other funds available through that lead agency can sometimes be used for Part C services.

Part B of the law provides funding to states to run special education. Most commonly, states do not directly administer services but local government does. Much of the federal funding is used to support school districts with guidance on specific disabilities or educational programs, with legal fees in cases of IDEA disputes, and on collecting formative and summative evaluation data.

Part D of the law provides funding for technical assistance, dissemination, and evaluation. Because inclusion is still being addressed in school districts, these efforts frequently address them, directly or indirectly.

States themselves provide funding for inclusive education. State funds are usually administered through local educational agencies (LEAs), which receive their funding mostly from the county or city they serve. Local funding, supplemented as it might be from state or federal funds, is largely responsible for funding general-education classrooms.

The next link in the chain is local government/schools, financed largely by taxes and, in some states, a lottery (i.e., a gaming system, in which participants buy tickets and hope their number is drawn). Because property and other taxes vary by district, some schools practicing inclusive education have plenty of funds and others have little.

Through all these funding streams, the extent to which inclusive education itself is funded, is hard to determine. The money tends to be appropriated for general or special education. If the mores of the general education in a given district or state command that children with disabilities are part of the classroom, funds might be used to make that possible. If the mores command that children with disabilities belong to special education, funds are less likely to be used to promote inclusion. A common question in education is: Whose child is this? This unfortunate question harks back to the two-bucket system: The presumed answer is that the child either belongs to general education or to special education. If the child belongs to the latter, general educators are less likely to consider it their responsibility to include the child.

The federal law supporting general education is called Every Student Succeeds Act (ESSA), which used to be called the Elementary and Secondary Education Act of 1965. The predecessor to ESSA was an act called No Child Left Behind, which was well known for making schools more accountable but also imposing unreasonable demands on them. ESSA requires that children with disabilities have to take the same assessments as other children, with one percent of all students (i.e., 10 % of students with disabilities) exempted; they take alternate assessments. The law also requires states to develop measures to combat bullying of students with disabilities, who are acknowledged to be at greater risk of bullying than are students without disabilities.

2.2.3. Competencies and qualifications of inclusive education teachers

Teachers working with children with disabilities in regular classrooms are, by and large, general educators. These teachers receive minimal training in working with children with disabilities. They might have taken a course or two in special education. Some training programs in early childhood education, however, are for dual licensure – that is, the training is in both general and special education. In the U.S., teachers have at least a bachelor's degree (four years of university education) and a state-administered teaching certificate.

General educators rely on help from special educators and therapists. The amount and quality of the consultation from these specialists varies (McWilliam, 1996).

2.2.4. What happens in an inclusive class

The assumptions of teachers working in inclusive classrooms range from isolation to true inclusion. The isolation occurs when the teacher ignores the child with disabilities, who has to manage on his or her own. This can obviously be a recipe for disaster, depending on the disability. Assuming the business of a classroom is teaching and learning, if the child has difficulty benefiting from teaching and difficulty learning, isolation will lead to failure. If the child has motor disabilities that do not impede his or her ability to handle learning materials such as books and computers, the child has a chance to succeed. Children with sensory disabilities (i.e. hearing or vision impairment) will not succeed without accommodations. True inclusion, at the other end of this range, means the entire classroom environment supports the participation of every child. Participation is a key word too infrequently invoked in education, unlike in health and disability studies. If the child can be engaged (i.e. meaningfully participating) in classroom routines, with all the help and accommodations that might take, he or she can succeed in the inclusive classroom (Aguiar, McWilliam, 2013; Rosenshine, Berliner, 1978).

Most schools have a resource room, which is the special education teacher's room. This room is where children deemed to be needing special instruction go for certain lessons. For example, professionals might consider a child to be unable to benefit from the regular mathematics lessons, so he or she goes to the resource room for this subject. One of the problems with the resource room is that special education teachers often have to be in their rooms at every lesson, thereby precluding them from collaborating with teachers during their planning times or during regular class times.

Another support for inclusion provided to children with disabilities is the individual assistant, usually a paraprofessional assigned to help the child in the regular-education classroom. This resource can make it possible for children with considerable needs to participate meaningfully in the classroom. Schools need to (a) determine who supervises the aide (regular or special educator), (b) ensure the aide does not become a VelcroTM aide (i.e., stuck to the student all the time), and (c) instead of using the aide as an extra pair of hands in the classroom, helping the target student only when necessary.

One accommodation which teachers can make for students with disabilities is to give them separate in-class or homework assignments. If the student can participate in the class activity but has difficulty doing the academic assignment given to the other students, this accommodation preserves the important aspect of participation.

A variation on this accommodation is to give the student an alternate form of the same assignment. For example, the class might be required to answer 20 questions, using completed sentences. The child with disabilities might be required to answer 10 questions using incomplete sentences, owing to his or her difficulty with writing.

A major gap in the knowledge of general educators is their lack of understanding of structured teaching or prompting strategies. Unfortunately,
special educators are becoming less knowledgeable about this content too.
Most teachers do not have the basic knowledge of behavioural concepts
of operant conditioning that underlie learning and teaching. They do not
know the difference between a task direction and a prompt, the importance of the timing of prompts, the different kinds of prompts, how to
fade prompts, shaping, chaining, whole-task teaching, task analysis, and
so on. These strategies are supposed to be at the core of teaching and
learning, especially with children with disabilities. Although the behavioural tradition has arguably been stronger in the U.S. than anywhere else,
the tradition is waning when it comes to use in classrooms. A renaissance
is badly needed, because most of the evidence for successful teaching of
children with disabilities, particularly autism and developmental disabilities, is behavioural (Lewis, Wheeler, Carter, 2017).

2.2.5. Barriers to the development of inclusive education

In addition to barriers mentioned above, two further barriers are the pressure of test preparation and insufficient collaborative consultation. With
the education establishment's obsession with outcomes, schools are testing
children often, and the results have high stakes for teachers and schools.
Therefore, teachers are under pressure to ensure their children do well on
these standardized tests. This pressure takes away the freedom sometimes
needed to pay extra attention to the struggling learner. Furthermore, the
test preparation activities might be the very kinds of activities the child with
learning disabilities, intellectual disabilities, or autism has trouble with.
Special education teachers could help. That, perhaps, is how they would
be best used – as supports to general education teachers. Unfortunately,
the two models most commonly adopted for the relationship between
these two types of teachers are rescue and recommend. Rescue involves
the special education teacher taking the child from the regular classroom
and teaching him or her in the resource room. Recommend involves the
special education teacher's giving suggestions to the general education
teacher. The problem with this model is that those suggestions might
not be the right ones or might be delivered badly, because the special

education teacher used an expert model of consultation (Kelleher, Riley-Tillman, Power, 2008). If special education teachers used collaborative consultation, involving asking many questions before issuing suggestions and involving the general education teacher in all aspects of intervention design, general education teachers would apply interventions and would do so with integrity.

2.2.6. The future of inclusive education

The future of inclusive education in the U.S. might depend on developing competencies of special education teachers, rigorous training of general educators, and a focus on engagement. Special education teachers, as mentioned earlier, need to be experts at collaborative consultation, incidental teaching, and prompting strategies. Incidental teaching is like scaffolding or expanding. It involves ensuring the child is engaged, following the child's lead, eliciting a more sophisticated form of the child's engaged behaviour, and ensuring the interaction was reinforcing (Casey, McWilliam, 2008; Casey, McWilliam, Sims, 2012). General education teachers also need rigorous training in ecobehavioural teaching strategies (Lee, Niileksela, 2014). This would ensure that they saw the path to learning through changing the environment in which the child learns, rather than thinking of the problem being in the child. This vision of learning leads to a focus on engagement. If all the professionals involved in the child's education understood that the child's engagement in daily routines, in the home, the classroom, and the community, were the keys to the child's learning and successful functioning, their approach to children would be individualized and therefore relevant (Almqvist, 2006; McWilliam, Casey, 2008).

Conclusion

The history of inclusive education in the United States paralleled efforts to provide greater opportunities to disenfranchised people. Although not always contemporary with changes in education of children with disabilities, the rights of women, minority races and ethnicities, and people with mental illness, the processes were similar. Essentially, advocates spoke up, laws were passed (with legal battles in pursuit), and societal views changed. Today, all Americans presumably know that children with disabilities are in the schools. They are at least in the right buildings, by and large. Within schools, the extent of inclusion varies, and the types of disabilities represented varies. Three areas still need attention. First, the special education system should move away from a reliance on diagnoses for placement and services and, instead, rely more on behavioural descriptors of learning and behaviour needs. This could allow schools to dispense with the two-bucket system of placement, it could make programming instruction more individualized, and, in early intervention, it could avoid the pernicious grasp of insurance companies, including the federal insurance system, where therapies are assigned on the basis of diagnosis. Second, partnerships with families should be established, so professionals help with the child's inclusion (i.e., engagement) in home and community routines. The current system is confined to the school building. Because the child spends more time out of the classroom than in it, professionals should build the capacity of the child's other caregivers. Third, schools should focus on normalization (Bailey, McWilliam, 1990; Bailey, McWilliam, Buysse, Wesley, 1998; Wolfensberger, 1970), so children and their families have the same opportunities as others. Bricker (2000) suggested schools refocus by "(a) ensuring that inclusion benefits all children and families, (b) improving understanding of which strategies and procedures work and which do not, and (c) improving the clarity of outcomes for individual children who participate in inclusion programs." To achieve more normalized education, the continued part-time segregation needs to be examined. Is the problem that the child cannot learn well in the environment or the environment is not prepared to teach the child well?

References

Aguiar, C., McWilliam, R. A. (2013). Consistency of toddler engagement across two settings. *Early Childhood Research Quarterly, 28*, 102–110.

Almqvist, L. (2006). Patterns of engagement in young children with and without developmental delay. *Journal of Policy and Practice in Intellectual Disabilities, 3*, 65–75.

Bailey, D. B., McWilliam, R. A. (1990). Normalizing early intervention. *Topics in Early Childhood Special Education, 10*, 33.

Bailey, D. B., McWilliam, R. A., Buysse, V., Wesley, P. W. (1998). Inclusion in the context of competing values in early childhood education. *Early Childhood Research Quarterly, 13,* 27–47.

Barry, B. (1998). Social exclusion, social isolation, and the distribution of income. Understanding social exclusion.

Bauwens, J., Hourcade, J. J., Friend, M. (1989). Cooperative teaching: A model for general and special education integration. *Remedial and Special Education, 10,* 17–22.

Bricker, D. (2000). Inclusion: How the scene has changed. *Topics in Early Childhood Special Education, 20,* 14–19.

Brown, L., Branston, M. B., Hamre-Nietupski, S., Pumpian, I., Certo, N., Gruenewald, L. (1979). A strategy for developing chronological-age-appropriate and functional curricular content for severely handicapped adolescents and young adults. *The Journal of Special Education, 13,* 81–90.

Buysse, V. (1993). Friendships of preschoolers with disabilities in community-based child care settings. *Journal of Early Intervention, 17,* 380–395.

Carlberg, C., Kavale, K. (1980). The efficacy of special versus regular class placement for exceptional children: A meta-analysis. *The Journal of Special Education, 14,* 295–309.

Casey, A. M., McWilliam, R. A. (2008). Graphical feedback to increase teachers' use of incidental teaching. *Journal of Early Intervention,* 251–268.

Casey, A. M., McWilliam, R. A., Sims, J. (2012). Contributions of incidental teaching, developmental quotient, and peer interactions to child engagement. *Infants & Young Children, 25,* 122–135.

Chalfant, J. C., Van Dusen Pysh, M. (1989). Teacher assistance teams: Five descriptive studies on 96 teams. *Remedial and Special Education, 10,* 49–58.

Clough, P., Corbett, J. (2000). Theories of inclusive education: A students' guide. London: Paul Chapman Publishing Ltd.

Datesman, M. K., Crandall, J. A., Kearny, E. N. (1997). The American ways: An introduction to American culture. Upper Saddlee River, NJ: Prentice Hall Regents.

Delquadri, J., Greenwood, C. R., Whorton, D., Carta, J. J., Hall, R. V. (1986). Classwide peer tutoring. *Exceptional Children, 52,* 535–542.

Deno, E. (1970). Cascade system of special education services. *Exceptional Children, 37,* 229–237.

Deno, E. (1970). Special education as developmental capital. *Exceptional Children, 37,* 229–237.

Deno, S. L. (1985). Curriculum-based measurement: The emerging alternative. *Exceptional Children, 52,* 219–232.

Dunn, L. M. (1968). Special education for the mildly retarded—Is much of it justifiable? *Exceptional Children, 35,* 5–22.

Edgar, E. (1987). Secondary programs in special education: Are many of them justifiable? *Exceptional Children, 53,* 555–561.

Epanchin, B. C., Friend, M. (2007). The adolescence of inclusive practices: Building bridges through collaboration. In: J. McLeskey (Ed.), Reflections on inclusion: Classic articles that shaped our thinking (pp. 213–219). Arlington, VA: Council for Exceptional Children.

Fletcher, J. M., Vaughn, S. (2009). Response to intervention: Preventing and remediating academic difficulties. *Child development perspectives, 3,* 30–37.

Fuchs, D., Fuchs, L. S. (1994). Inclusive schools movement and the radicalization of special education reform. *Exceptional Children, 60,* 294–309.

Fuchs, D., Fuchs, L. S. (2012). Competing visions for educating students with disabilities: Inclusion versus full inclusion. *Childhood Education, 74,* 309–316.

Giangreco, M. F., Dennis, R., Cloninger, C., Edelman, S., Schattman, R. (1993). "I've counted Jon": Transformational experiences of teachers educating students with disabilities. *Exceptional Children, 59,* 359–372.

Gidley, J., Hampson, G., Wheeler, L., Bereded-Samuel, E. (2010). Social inclusion: Context, theory and practice. The Australasian *Journal of University-Community Engagement, 5,* 6–36.

Haager, D. (2007). Classroom instruction in inclusive settings. In: J. McLeskey (Ed.), Reflections on inclusion: Classic articles that shaped our thinking (pp. 25–254). Arlingto, VA: Council for Exceptional Children.

Idol, L., Nevin, A., Paolucci-Whitcomb, P. (1994). Collaborative consultation (2nd ed.). Austin, TX: PRO-ED.

Jimerson, S. R., Burns, M. K., VanDerHeyden, A. M. (2015). Handbook of response to intervention: The science and practice of multi-tiered systems of support. New York: Springer.

Kauffman, J. M. (1993). How we might achieve the radical reform of special education. *Exceptional Children, 60,* 6–16.

Kauffman, J. M., Hallahan, D. P. (1995). The illusion of full inclusion: A comprehensive critique of a current special education bandwagon: ERIC.

Kelleher, C., Riley-Tillman, T. C., Power, T. J. (2008). An initial comparison of collaborative and expert-driven consultation on treatment integrity. *Journal of Educational and Psychological Consultation, 18,* 294–324.

Kochhar-Bryant, C. A. (2007). Inclusion in secondary schools. In: J. McLeskey (Ed.), Reflections on inclusion: Classic articles that shaped our thinking (pp. 283–285). Arlington, VA: Council for Exceptional Children.

Lee, S. W., Niileksela, C. R. (2014). Ecobehavioral consultation in school-based problem-solving teams. In: Ecobehavioral Consultation in Schools (pp. 177–197). London: Routledge.

Lewis, R. B., Wheeler, J. J., Carter, S. L. (2017). Teaching students with special needs in general education classrooms. New York: Pearson.

MacMillan, D. L., Gresham, F. M., Forness, S. R. (1996). Full inclusion: An empirical perspective. *Behavioral Disorders, 21,* 145–159.

McLeskey, J. (2007). Reflections on inclusion: Classic articles that shaped our thinking. Arlington, VA: Council for Exceptional Children.

McLeskey, J., Waldron, N. L., So, T.-s. H., Swanson, K., Loveland, T. (2001). Perspectives of teachers toward inclusive school programs. *Teacher Education and Special Education, 24,* 108–115.

McWilliam, R. A. (2011). The top 10 mistakes in early intervention—and the solutions. *Zero to Three, 31,* 11–16.

McWilliam, R. A. (Ed.) (1996). Rethinking pull-out services in early intervention: A professional resource. Baltimore, MD: Paul H. Brookes Publishing Co.

McWilliam, R. A., Casey, A. M. (2008). Engagement of every child in the preschool classroom. Baltimore, MD: Paul H. Brookes Co.

National Commission on Excellence in Education. (1983). A nation at risk: The imperative for educational reform. *The Elementary School Journal,* 84, 113–130.

Odom, S. L., Buysse, V., Soukakou, E. (2011). Inclusion for young children with disabilities: A quarter century of research perspectives. *Journal of Early Intervention,* 33, 344–356.

Rafferty, Y., Boettcher, C., Griffin, K. W. (2001). Benefits and risks of reverse inclusion for preschoolers with and without disabilities: Parents' perspectives. *Journal of Early Intervention,* 24, 266–286.

Reynolds, M. C., Wang, M. C., Walberg, H. J. (1987). The necessary restructuring of special and regular education. *Exceptional Children,* 53, 391–398.

Rosenshine, B. V., Berliner, D. C. (1978). Academic engaged time. *Journal of Education and Teaching,* 4, 3–16.

Salend, S., Garrick-Duhaney, L. M. (2007). Research related to inclusion and program Effectiveness: Yesterday, today and tomorrow. In: Reflections on inclusion: Classic articles that shaped our thinking (pp. 147–159). Arlington, VA: Council for Exceptional Children.

Schumm, J. S., Vaughn, S. (1991). Making adaptations for mainstreamed students: General classroom teachers' perspectives. *Remedial and Special Education,* 12, 18–27.

Scruggs, T. E., Mastropieri, M. A. (1996). Teacher perceptions of mainstreaming/inclusion, 1958–1995: A research synthesis. *Exceptional Children,* 63, 59–74.

Stainback, W., Stainback, S. (1984). A rationale for the merger of special and regular education. *Exceptional Children,* 51, 102–111.

Sullivan, A. L., Bal, A. (2013). Disproportionality in special education: Effects of individual and school variables on disability risk. *Exceptional Children,* 79, 475–494.

U.S. Department of Education – Office of Special Education and Rehabilitative Services – Office of Special Education Programs. (2017). 39TH annual report to Congress on the implementation of the Individuals with Disabilities Education Act, 2017. U.S. Department of Education. Washington, DC.

Wagner, M., Newman, L., Cameto, R., Javitz, H., Valdes, K. (2012). A national picture of parent and youth participation in IEP and transition planning meetings. *Journal of Disability Policy Studies, 23*, 140–155.

Waldron, N. (2007). Reflecting on Teacher Attitudes. In: J. McLeskey (Ed.), Reflections on inclusion (pp. 183–187). Arlington, VA: Council for Exceptional Children.

Will, M. C. (1986). Educating children with learning problems: A shared responsibility. *Exceptional Children, 52*, 411–415.

Wolfensberger, W. (1970). The principle of normalization and its implications to psychiatric services. *American Journal of Psychiatry, 127*, 291–297.

Wolfensberger, W. (1983). Social role valorization: A proposed new term for the principle of normalization. *Mental Retardation, 21*, 234–239.

Woods, J. J., Wilcox, M. J., Friedman, M., Murch, T. (2011). Collaborative consultation in natural environments: Strategies to enhance family-centered supports and services. *Language, speech, and hearing services in schools, 42*, 379–392.

World Health Organization. (2007). International classification of functioning, disability, and health: Children & youth version: ICF-CY. Geneva: World Health Organization.

Zhang, C., Bennett, T. (2003). Facilitating the meaningful participation of culturally and linguistically diverse families in the IFSP and IEP process. *Focus on Autism and Other Developmental Disabilities, 18*, 51–60.

Miloň Potměšil

Chapter 3 Inclusive education in the Czech Republic

3.1 Theoretical foundations of inclusive education

Terminology

This chapter concerns the field of special pedagogy in the Czech Republic, which is a very good example of an interdisciplinary approach within the wider context of pedagogy and education. At first, it seems necessary to clarify the terminology of the key concepts that will be used here. The most important concepts are normalization, integration and inclusion. The most significant statement as regards the education of children was delivered by the representatives of 92 UNESCO member states in the 1994 declaration[1], promoting the effort to remove any discriminatory attitudes through the introduction of open inclusive schools and to influence public awareness of the principle of inclusion.

An important component of this was *normalization*, which is a partial requirement of adjusting conditions to ensure a "normal" life for intellectually disabled people. Normalization was first introduced by a Danish lawyer Niels Erik Bank-Mikkelsen. This concept was further developed mostly in northern European countries and it became a set of principles which could be implemented into practice by other countries. These principles comprised the basic perspective, which ensured that the adjustment of the environment and the attitudes of the general public should be executed in such a way that they are harmonized with the needs of the disabled. The adjustments required in the context of normalization are related to

---

1 The Salamanca Statement and Framework for Action on Special Needs Education World Conference on Special Needs Education: Access and Quality, Salamanca, Spain, June 7–10, 1994, United Nations Educational, Scientific and Cultural Organization, Ministry of Education and Science, Spain.

everyday activities and engagement in normal social life at a level which is satisfactory for individual disabled people. This concept has also become the basis of a similar approach to the process of educating and socializing disabled individuals in general.

One of the most frequently applied concepts in special education is *integration*. A definition of this term can be found in the documents of almost every nation's ministry of education. However, it is usually limited to mentioning only individual and group integration.

Another concept, the most important in the context of this study, is *inclusion*. Czech sources do not always clarify the difference between *integration* and *inclusion*. For instance, Průcha (1998) defines inclusion in education as a result of the movement striving for establishing integrated education for even severely disabled individuals. In the publications focused on present-day pedagogy, both these concepts are used only to a limited extent – for instance, in Průcha (2002). The concept of inclusion is related to a shift in the paradigm of special pedagogy (Forlin, 2006), the first steps in this field in the Czech Republic were taken by Jesenský (1995, 1998). It is necessary here to return to the Salamanca conference in Spain, where inclusion became a key concept. Its declaration mentions the programmes focused on the education of disabled learners within the framework of mainstream schools. It also emphasizes the principle of individualization in content planning and the pace of education, as well as the requirements for adjustment to the school environment, in which the entire educational process takes place.

As mentioned above, this approach led to a shift in the paradigm of special pedagogy, which subsequently became a comprehensive pedagogical discipline. Compared to the previous ideation of disability, viewed rather from the medical perspective, special education is currently regarded as an ancillary discipline aimed at preparing the disabled for life in society – namely the highest achievable quality of life, as close as possible to the standards of the majority – the population without disability.

For the purpose of this text, it is necessary to summarize the basic difference between integration and inclusion, which lies in differing notions of children or learners. From the perspective of integration, the differences between a group of disabled children and a group of fully abled children are respected – the main effort is to engage or bring the two different groups of children together (regarding their physical conditions or educational needs) in the context of education, and to provide them with special-pedagogical support where necessary. In contrast, inclusive education views children or learners from a perspective which disregards differences in the above-mentioned elements – it presumes that every member of a given group has some individual needs.

As regards the Czech context, the relationship between integration and inclusion was defined by Kocurová (2002) in the following way:

> Integration – focus on the needs of an individual with disability; specialist expertise; special interventions; benefits for the integrated learner; specific adjustment of the environment; focus on the disabled learner being educated; assessment of the learner by a specialist.
> Inclusion – focus on the needs of all the educated children; expertise of standard teachers; education convenient for everyone; benefits for all learners; general adjustment of school; focus on the group and school; the teacher's general strategy; assessment by the teacher; focus on educational parameters.

The objectives of the educational process are determined by the national curriculum and subsequently by the school's education curriculum and by an individual syllabus, if necessary depending on the learner's specific needs. Modern educational philosophy perceives the current trend as comprehensive (for children of all abilities) within the framework of general pedagogy. For instance, Barrow and Woods (2006) dealt with the requirements imposed on pedagogy and teachers implementing the process of education which they characterized as "rational" and they explain further this modern approach to pedagogy and the necessary professional training of teachers. A teachers' ideal skill set for work with disabled children and learners is described by Brue and Wilmshurst (2005), who made a list of the skills necessary for a teacher to work with children with various disabilities and therefore also with special educational needs. In "The Rehabilitation Act of 1973," particularly in Section 504, requirements for teachers are specified through the strategies which are focused on, for instance: organizing the educational process, manifestations of behaviour, adjustments to the environment and conditions, etc. Inclusion and inclusive education were described by Hull et al. (2002), who formulated the following fundamental assumptions:

- Disabled children can implement in the same syllabuses as their peers.
- They can attend the environment corresponding to their current age.
- They can make use of the individual approach in the form of an individual educational plan if needed.
- They are entitled to special-pedagogical support tailored to their needs.

In their publication, the authors consider the requirements for teachers working under the conditions of inclusion. Apart from practical skills, the article also points to other prerequisites deemed necessary to work in such a specific occupation. The authors concluded that in the case of inclusive education (and integrated education as well) the number of requirements and the range of pedagogical competences extend to an unprecedented scope. This deals with raising and educating disabled children and learners alongside their fully abled peers. Therefore, the readiness and skills of the pedagogical staff must be considered. Hájková (2005) defines professional teaching skills in the Czech context as the sum of prerequisites for the performance of pedagogical activity, as well as the capacity to act in an intelligent way in situations that are constantly new and unique, aiming to find an appropriate reaction on the spot. A teacher possessing the abilities to assess and decide can find appropriate reactions in situations which are new and unpredictable.

In this text, there is no intension to introduce specific skill sets that may be required for teachers educating disabled children (depending on the kind of disability). This chapter only provides an illustrative example of the requirements needed to educate a child with hearing impairment. Apart from the ability to communicate in spoken Czech as well as in sign language at a level which does not limit the process of education by a communication barrier, teachers should be prepared for the following: emotional literacy – introduction into the theory and practice of emotional life, concepts and descriptions of individual emotions and experiences; self-control – conscious behaviour motivated by a previously determined aim; social competence – the establishment and development of age-appropriate social skills which reflect the culture and environment in which the child lives; development of good relationships with peers – practice and development of social skills in a peer group; and problem solving skills for interpersonal relationships. A definition of the scope of the knowledge is deliberately omitted here, as it is standardized in the national curriculum (Potměšil, 2007).

The results of a study conducted in Iceland by Bjarnason (2005) show that adjusting conditions during the shift from the traditional approach to inclusive education is also reflected in the training of future teachers. With regard to the competences and attitudes dealt with in this text, the author discusses the "changed general educator's roles in the face of growing student diversity."

Inclusive education or rather integrated education in the Czech environment is embedded in the legislation (č. 561/2004 Sb., 27/2016 Sb., 72/2005 Sb.) and implemented in practice. There are various forms and methods of work related to these forms of education which are further determined by the options at a particular school.

Historical background of education for the disabled in the Czech National Conception

One of the leading personalities driving the modern concept of special pedagogy, particularly in speech therapy and teaching learners with hearing impairment, was Miloš Sovák. As originally an otorhinolaryngologist, he focused on the prevention of and intervention into disorders and defects and gradually specialized in rehabilitation and education. He was active in the field of defectology, mainly from the mid-1940s to the 1990s. He established the Department of Defectology at Charles University and his achievements also comprise a significant contribution to the modern concept of special pedagogy. Besides his work on the development of this scientific field, he also focused on the historical development of care for disabled people – therefore, his work also provides a description of the development of such care (Sovák, 1980).

Slovák characterizes its individual phases from the perspective of historical and social formations. Chronologically, the first phase of his classification is the **repressive phase**, where people with a defect or those functioning insufficiently were rejected or even killed. In the next phase, these individuals were exploited and used as slaves. A **charitable approach** to the disabled brought into the society by Christianity. According to Sovák, this innovation is reflected in the turn of humanity towards disabled people and accepting them as **part of the human society**. The development of technology and the labour market resulted in a need for increasingly employable population, which is, according to Sovák, associated with the phase of **rehabilitation** of the disabled. Another objective was also to reduce the care expenses related to disabled people by increasing their independence. The phase of socialist political establishment involved centralism and centralized care for the disabled with the possibility of their social engagement both in work and culture. This phase was also characterized by certain attention to preventing the consequences of disability in the form of special pedagogy, which was, however, conducted under ideologically motivated supervision. Thus, **socialization** proceeded in accordance to centralized plans. To conclude this section, one may say that it was the medical professional profile of Professor Sovák which strengthened the approach towards the disabled as a group of non-healthy people. This **medical model** is grounded on the presence of a defect and a disability. The fundamental principle lies here in describing differences from the normal state within the population. The key terms of this principle are: diagnosis, assessment, treatment, medical care, rehabilitation, and re-education.

Jesenský (2000) proposed some adjustment to Sovák's concept, elaborating the theory into phases of development in the care for and attitude towards disabled people.

Early Middle Antiquity is characterized as a phase of repression and rejection. Disabled people were regarded as a burden to the survival of relatives or the tribe, and as such they were rejected, killed, or abandoned. A characteristic feature of the later Antiquity was the exploitation of disabled people and their non-impaired functions.

In the Medieval society, Christianity brought about charity and relationships based on love for one's fellows. In practice, this meant ensuring basic needs, including the provision of an asylum.

The next phase was the Renaissance with its philanthropic approach to people in general and thus to the disabled as well. This phase is followed by the Enlightenment period where a human was defined in respect to nature and there was an increasing interest in humans and the prerequisites for functioning within society. The human being was the focus of science and philosophy – and so were disabled people. This period was also characterized by an increased interest in the satisfaction of higher needs and the consequent enhancement (from the modern perspective) of the quality of life.

The phase between the 1800s and 1900s was influenced by the advancement in learning and social life, and by an increased interest in people from the economic perspective as necessary workforce, which involved the disabled and people affected by war. The main reasons for developments in education and increased care for disabled people were their employability and the possibly most intensive participation in the economic development of society. In order to fulfil the life needs of those unable to work, special institutions were established. In both categories – education and social care – the focus on disabled people gradually increased; in practice, however, they were based on the principle of segregation.

The second half of the 20th century and the turn of the 21st century brought a change in the quality of interpersonal relationships. General knowledge and cultural development were the basis of the Postmodern Age. Postmodernism affected the entire range of human activity and influenced upbringing and education as well. In this context, the progress in the Czechoslovak Socialist Republic (CSSR), largely influenced by the contemporary political system, was slow and dependent on communist ideology and the consent of the Soviet Union.

Western Europe proceeded very quickly in enhancing the quality of care for different and weaker individuals. This also involved education and social care. For instance, an institute for total communication was founded in Copenhagen in 1972, while in the CSSR the first article by a "brave" teacher of the deaf appeared as late as 1985. In addition, it was published in a journal intended primarily for deaf readers and thus achieved minimal publicity. Open discussion on the alternatives of communication in educating learners with hearing impairment was only possible after the revolutionary changes in 1989. This is an example of the situation in education and care for disabled persons. The end of the 20th century was characterized by the search and transformation to incorporate the whole of the society. The rights of the disabled were formulated so as to grant them possibly the biggest independence. The support from fully abled people developed at both the individual, voluntary level and the national level, embedded in legislation.

The transition to a new millennium was influenced in this respect by continuously accelerating technical advancement, which positively influenced the development of technical compensatory aids. Moreover, inclusion became an increasingly promoted approach to the education of disabled learners. In addition to the promotion of inclusion in the context of the entire society, at the Czech national level – legislative and methodological documents are created, providing the basis for implementation of the inclusive approach in education. The framework for the national version was established by EU documents, which were functionally implemented in Western Europe. In the Czech Republic, more time is needed for adaptation of the society and the educational system.

3.2. Inclusive education in practice in the Czech Republic (2018)

The educational system in the Czech Republic

The present education system is structured and enables high permeability between the individual levels. In accordance with the International Standard Classification of Education – ISCED (2013), the education system is divided as follows:

1. pre-primary education (early childhood education, nursery school, kindergarten)
2. primary education – basic education (first stage of primary school, year 1–5)
3. lower secondary education – second stage of primary school (year 6–9), including general secondary schools (*gymnázium*) and conservatories
4. higher secondary education – (year 10–13); secondary schools, secondary technical schools, general secondary schools, conservatories, etc.
5. post-secondary schools – post-secondary study
6. tertiary professional schools
7. universities – Bachelor's and Master's degree of study
8. doctoral degree courses.

State education in the Czech Republic

As regards administration, schools in the Czech Republic may be public (state), private or religious. Public education is governed by the Ministry of Education, Youth and Sports (MŠMT), which supervises the state budget financing, the quality of education, qualification-related requirements for teachers, and the scope and content of the curriculum at each level of the educational system. State authorities establish and govern schools at the regional or municipal level. Secondary schools, conservatories and tertiary professional schools fall under the charge of regional authority. Nursery and primary schools are established at the municipal level. Education at all levels is governed by the centrally issued educational curricula; these are further elaborated by schools to form school curricula with regard to the conditions at every particular school. Curricula for tertiary professional schools and universities are accredited by the National Accreditation Bureau. Universities are autonomous institutions and their independence from the state provides them with a high level of academic freedom. Private and religious schools may operate upon the consent of the state.

Pre-primary education

The age limit for beginning pre-primary education is 3 years. On the 1st of September 2017, obligatory education was enacted for children from the age of 5 – in the last year before they begin the obligatory primary school education. This right may be used even by parents of four-year-olds.

Primary school

School attendance is obligatory at primary schools and covers nine years of education. After completing their fifth or seventh year of primary school, some students may continue their study at multi-year general secondary schools if they pass the entrance examination.

Secondary schools

After the completion of the primary school, pupils may apply to study at a secondary school ended by the *"maturita"* (school leaving) exam – this refers to secondary technical schools or general secondary schools. Having passed the unified entrance examination, they begin their attendance, which usually covers four years. The study programme is concluded with the *maturita* exam consisting of the state part obligatory for all students and the school part profiled according to the type of the particular study programme. At schools which are not ended with the *maturita* exam, studying is concluded by the unified apprenticeship exam. Secondary-level education at schools not ended by the *maturita* exam also includes on-the-job apprenticeships either in a common four-year secondary school, or as post-secondary and qualification extension studies.

Tertiary education

Tertiary professional schools and universities provide the option of professionally or academically oriented education. According to the Ministry of Education, 30.1 % of the population completed tertiary education in 2015. Educational courses at tertiary professional schools cover three years. University studies are usually structured into Bachelor's (3 years), the Master's (2 years), and the Doctoral (4 years) levels. Some fields of study are provided in non-structured study programmes – Master's studies which take 4, 5, or 6 years (e.g., medicine).

Inclusive education

Education is legislatively regulated by the Education Act with Amendment No. 82/2015 Coll., which also defines inclusive education at the levels of pre-primary, primary, secondary and tertiary professional education. In particular, it defines a learner with special educational needs: "A child, learner or university student with special educational needs is a person in need of supportive measures in order to accomplish their educational potential or to exercise their right on an equal basis with others. Supportive measures are necessary adjustments to education and school services corresponding to the child's, learner's or student's physical condition, culture environment or other life conditions. A child, learner or student is entitled to free of charge supportive measures provided by a particular school and school facilities."

Supportive measures defined in the context of the above-mentioned students involve special advisory services, adjustments to organization, methods and forms of education, and the possibility of extending study by up to two years. Adjustments may also involve the conditions for admission and completion of education, usage of compensatory aids and special didactic materials, adaptation to the expected educational outcomes, education according to an individual educational plan, and the services of a teaching assistant or an interpreter, as well as technical adjustment to the environment based on the nature of the special educational needs of a learner. The category of learners with special educational needs also comprises talented learners.

Supportive measures are organizational in their nature; they are implemented by modification of the methods, forms and contents of education. At the secondary and higher levels of the educational system, they include the possibility of extending the length of study by up to two years. Supportive measures also include external support of advisory organs – usually at special pedagogy centres or pedagogical-psychological counselling centres. The accessibility of mainstream education is also ensured by the use of compensatory and educational aids and communication approaches including the option of using an interpreter for the Czech sign language or a teaching assistant. Counselling organs participate in creating the individual educational plans (IEP – IVP).

These supportive measures are classified into five levels according to organizational, pedagogical and financial demands. Individual types or levels of supportive measures may be combined. Supportive measures on a higher level may be used if a school advisory office decides that the lower level of supportive measures are not sufficient to enable the fulfilment of the learner's educational potential and to ensure their right to education, with regard to the nature of the special educational needs of the particular child, learner or student or to the progress and results of the provision of supportive measures already applied. The classification of supportive measures into individual levels is determined by the relevant legislation.

Supportive measures – level I

Supportive measures at the first level may be implemented by a school or educational facility even without any recommendation of an advisory organ. Supportive measures at the second to fifth level may be implemented only upon recommendation of a school advisory office. Instead of the recommended supportive measure, a school or an educational facility may also implement a different measure of the same level after consulting the particular school advisory office and with a prior written consent of an adult learner, or a legal guardian of a child, unless it is contrary to the interest of the learner.

Supportive measures – levels II–V

To provide supportive measures at the second to fifth level by a school or educational facility, a prior written consent of an adult learner, or the legal guardian of a child is always required. For children and students in need of education in a different communication system (sign language or a different form of communication), specific support is ensured at a qualified level, including techniques within the system of augmentative and alternative communication. The provision of supportive measures may be terminated upon a recommendation of a school advisory office if the measures cease to be purposeful.

For children and students with mental and physical disabilities, sight or hearing impairment, severe speech impairment, severe developmental learning disorders, severe developmental behavioural disorders, multiple disabilities, and autism, special schools, classes, departments and study groups may be established. The admission of a child or student defined as above into such a class, study group, department or school is possible only if the school advisory office decides that the supportive measures would not be sufficient to enable the fulfilment of the educational potential of a learner and to execute their right to education with regard to the nature of their special educational needs or to the progress and results of the supportive measures already provided. For admission, a written application from an adult learner, or a legal guardian of a child, as well as a recommendation of a school advisory office, compliant with the interest of a learner are required. Establishing a class, department or study group as defined above is only possible upon the consent of the Ministry in the case of schools established by the Ministry, registered churches or religious societies entitled to execute the special right to establish religious schools. In the case of other schools, a consent of the regional authority is necessary.

School advisory facilities and their role in inclusive education

School advisory facilities may provide counselling services to learners or to their legal guardians. Counselling aid may be provided to the above defined target group following the decision of the public authority. Prior to the entitlement of a learner to a supportive measure, a school or an educational facility collaborates particularly with the school advisory office, the respective educational authority, the medical doctor and the authority in charge of social and legal protection of children. The advisors' opinions are formulated in a report including a list and a description of the forms of the granted supportive measures and the related rules. The report is submitted to the counselling commissioner.

Education of talented learners

For talented children and students, the conditions which enable adequate development of their potential are created in schools and educational facilities. These conditions involve extended teaching of certain school subjects or adjustments to the daily regime for the learners participating in sport training within classes with extended physical training. Talented students have the opportunity to advance to a higher year without having to complete the requirements of the previous year upon a request issued by them or their legal guardians. A statement by a school advisory office and the registering provider of medical services in the field of general paediatric and adolescent medicine (hereinafter "the registering doctor") are necessary for this request. The necessary condition for the advancement is taking an exam covering all or part of the curriculum from the missed year by the learner. The contents and the extent of the exam are specified by the headmaster.

Individual educational plan

Upon a written recommendation of a school advisory office, the head-master may allow education according to an individual educational plan to an underage learner with special educational needs or with an exceptional talent, based on the request of their legal guardians, and to an adult student with special educational needs or with an exceptional talent based on their own request. The individual educational plan includes a detailed definition, organization and description of the purpose of supportive measures. It also determines the conditions for the use of a teaching assistant and the rules for the assistant's activity. A written consent for the provision of supportive measures, which has to be submitted as a record of parents' or guardians' awareness, is of great importance. Furthermore, the individual educational plan includes the rules and requirements concerning the identification of educational needs of talented learners and specifies the organization, admission, process and completion of their education and the rules for advancing to a higher year. The headmaster of the particular school takes responsibility for the existence of an individual educational plan, which should be elaborated in collaboration with the school advisory office.

The current quantification indicators of education in the Czech Republic

The recent surveys point to a significant, positive change in the educational level of the inhabitants of the Czech Republic. This fact is documented by a dramatic decrease in the number of citizens with primary education: in 1950 it amounted to 83 %, while in 2011 it was only 19 %. In contrast, the number of citizens with higher education increased from 1 % in 1950 to 19 % in 2011. Another significant change has taken place in the structure of citizens with secondary education. This process is also closely related to the mortality of elderly citizens with mostly primary education (Table 9).

Table 9. Highest educational attainment of population aged 15+ by 1950–2011 censuses (source: ČSÚ 1970; 2003; 2011)

Highest educational attainment of population aged 15+ by 1950–2011 censuses

Highest educational attainment	*Census year*[1]						
	1950	1961	1970[2]	1980	1991	2001	2011
Population total							
Total	6,757,757	7,142,962	7,700,993	7,879,910	8,137,779	8,575,198	8,947,632
Basic[3]	5,606,019	5,743,688	4,086,749	3,511,734	2,696,065	1,975,109	1,571,602
Secondary without A-level examination, technical	660,949	546,852	2,225,013	2,556,344	2,878,645	3,255,400	2,952,112
- apprentice schools	.	.	.	1,991,805	2,465,901	1,760,708	.
- technical schools	.	.	.	564,539	412,744	1,494,692	.
Secondary with A-level examination, general	141,528	205,352	260,111	278,303	342,506	430,982	610,759
Secondary with A-level examination, technical	194,872	437,473	773,997	1,058,352	1,515,339	1,703,935	1,814,305
- apprentice schools	.	.	.	10,572	95,540	125,281	.
- technical schools	.	.	.	1,047,780	1,419,799	1,578,654	.
Follow-up courses	.	.	.	.	.	188,114	247,937
Tertiary technical[4]	.	.	9,828	11,798	9,138	108,140	117,111
Higher education (university)	69,914	156,412	263,127	393,524	582,849	762,459	1,114,731
No school education	21,673	24,478	22,226	20,061	27,778	37,932	42,384
Not identified	62,802	28,707	59,942	49,794	85,459	113,127	476,691
Total	3,238,960	3,398,933	3,669,300	3,753,562	3,891,886	4,133,067	4,345,817
Males							
Basic[3]	2,583,731	2,652,461	1,439,426	1,269,447	961,720	683,077	579,016

Continued on next page

Table 9. Continued

Highest educational attainment of population aged 15+ by 1950–2011 censuses

	1950	1961	1970	1980	1991	2001	2011
Secondary without A-level examination, technical	335,931	248,972	1,466,502	1,543,138	1,679,506	1,873,383	1,703,103
- apprentice schools	.	.	.	1,332,200	1,539,704	1,062,279	.
- technical schools	.	.	.	210,938	139,802	811,104	.
Secondary with A-level examination, general	93,014	113,109	118,510	117,813	129,213	153,399	219,972
Secondary with A-level examination, technical	132,968	239,072	414,612	523,064	697,821	786,394	849,070
- apprentice schools	.	.	.	7,999	67,042	82,561	.
- technical schools	.	.	.	515,065	630,779	703,833	.
Follow-up courses	.	.	8,861	9,431	5,252	63,645	88,213
Tertiary technical[4]	.	.	.	.	.	50,014	43,061
Higher education (university)	59,192	123,655	186,610	260,336	365,162	445,380	577,685
No school education	8,593	9,457	8,745	8,140	12,039	16,483	19,698
Not identified	25,531	12,207	26,034	22,193	41,173	61,292	265,999
Total	**3,518,797**	**3,744,029**	**4,031,693**	**4,126,348**	**4,245,893**	**4,442,131**	**4,601,815**
Females							
Basic[3]	3,022,288	3,091,227	2,647,323	2,242,287	1,734,345	1,292,032	992,586
Secondary without A-level examination, technical	325,018	297,880	758,511	1,013,206	1,199,139	1,382,017	1,249,009
- apprentice schools	.	.	.	659,605	926,197	698,429	.
- technical schools	.	.	.	353,601	272,942	683,588	.
Secondary with A-level examination, general	48,514	92,243	141,601	160,490	213,293	277,583	390,787

Secondary with A-level examination, technical	61,904	198,401	359,385	535,288	817,518	917,541	965,235
- apprentice schools	.	.	.	2,573	28,498	42,720	.
- technical schools	.	.	.	532,715	789,020	874,821	.
Follow-up courses	.	.	.	.	.	124,469	159,724
Tertiary technical[3]	.	.	967	2,367	3,886	58,126	74,050
Higher education (university)	10,722	32,757	76,517	133,188	217,687	317,079	537,046
No school education	13,080	15,021	13,481	11,921	15,739	21,449	22,686
Not identified	37,271	16,500	33,908	27,601	44,286	51,835	210,692

3) Including incomplete basic education.

Table 10. Disabled learners in special primary schools for the disabled in 2015/16 (according to the region) (Source: www.uiv.cz)

		No. of schools	No. of learners	No. of girls
Czech Republic		349	22,721	8,382
	Capital City of Prague	36	3,031	1,035
	Central Bohemian Region	43	2,258	862
	South Bohemian Region	24	1,164	462
	Plzeň Region	19	1,333	482
	Karlovy Vary Region	10	640	236
	Ústí Region	26	2,354	897
Sub-category	Liberec Region	22	1,428	550
	Hradec Králové Region	26	1,513	541
	Pardubice Region	17	973	376
	Vysočina Region	14	764	304
	South Moravian Region	29	1,994	734
	Olomouc Region	25	1,721	634
	Zlín Region	23	1,017	343
	Moravian-Silesian Region	35	2,531	926

Primary education

At present, there is an increasing tendency in the admission of learners to primary education at mainstream schools while admission to primary schools for the disabled has been decreasing, as shown by the data from the annual statistical survey of the Ministry of Education of the Czech Republic. With regard to the number of students educated under Section 41 of the Education Act (education according to an individual educational plan), an increase may be observed at mainstream primary schools (Tables 10, 11).

At present, there is a tendency to integrate learners with different types of disabilities into mainstream primary schools. The integration of individuals with all types of disabilities has been increasing. With regard to the implemented inclusive education, it may be presumed that this increasing tendency will continue. The inclusive type of education came into effect on 1st September 2016. Table 10 illustrates the numbers of disabled learners

Table 11. Disabled learners in special classes and individually integrated in mainstream primary schools in 2016/2017 (according to the region) (Source: www.uiv.cz)

Area		Disabled learners								
		Total			in special classes			individually integrated		
		No. of schools	No. of learners		No. of schools	No. of learners		No. of schools	No. of learners	
			Total	girls only		total	girls only		total	girls only
Czech Republic	CZ0	3,737	81,644	25,992	533	28,438	10,345	3,384	53,206	15,647
Capital City of Prague	CZ010	243	8,887	2,887	45	3,525	1,193	206	5,362	1,694
Sub-category Central Bohemian Region	CZ020	506	10,634	3,239	61	2,909	1,068	463	7,725	2,171
South Bohemian Region	CZ031	219	2,713	918	28	1,211	476	195	1,502	442
Plzeň Region	CZ032	205	4,489	1,426	31	1,593	564	186	2,896	862
Karlovy Vary Region	CZ041	101	2,927	943	22	1,126	427	91	1,801	516
Ústí Region	CZ042	266	8,242	2,717	57	3,474	1,289	238	4,768	1,428
Liberec Region	CZ051	185	3,599	1,235	34	1,719	670	163	1,880	565
Hradec Králové Region	CZ052	248	5,692	1,903	34	1,627	577	222	4,065	1,326
Pardubice Region	CZ053	217	4,023	1,249	21	1,043	395	200	2,980	854
Vysočina Region	CZ063	216	4,024	1,292	27	1,143	432	202	2,881	860
South Moravian Region	CZ064	409	6,892	2,189	50	2,613	944	380	4,279	1,245
Olomouc Region	CZ071	270	4,916	1,498	33	1,939	700	245	2,977	798
Zlín Region	CZ072	234	3,413	1,020	30	1,203	403	211	2,210	617
Moravian-Silesian Region	CZ080	418	11,193	3,476	60	3,313	1,207	382	7,880	22

in mainstream primary schools in 2009/2010 – 2014/2015. The table presents the total numbers of learners integrated into mainstream primary schools with the distinction into individually integrated learners and learners educated in special. The data show positive progress from group to individual integration.

The total population of the Czech Republic in December 2017 was 10,555,930.

Secondary education

Education in secondary schools – disabled learners/girls according to the form of integration at mainstream schools (www.uiv.cz)

Table 12. Disabled learners in mainstream secondary schools (according to the form of integration) (Source: www.uiv.cz)

Area	Disabled learners total			in special classes				individually integrated		
	No. of schools	No. of learners total	girls only	No. of schools	No. of classes	No. of learners total	girls only	No. of schools	No. of learners total	girls only
Czech Republic	901	14,726	4,954	88	503	4,244	1,661	882	10,482	3,293
Capital City of Prague	87	1,650	458	6	35	347	75	87	1,303	383
Central Bohemia Region	108	1,980	581	16	78	662	218	105	1,318	363
South Bohemian Region	48	609	191	7	38	271	120	47	338	71
Plzeň Region	38	343	102	0	0	0	0	38	343	102
Karlovy Vary Region	37	592	169	6	14	90	16	35	502	153
Ústí Region	79	1,157	375	7	24	212	74	79	945	301
Liberec Region	30	427	146	2	14	131	53	30	296	93
Hradec Králové Region	58	989	368	7	39	398	167	52	591	201
Pardubice Region	49	1,023	355	4	63	328	134	49	695	221
Vysočina Region	48	703	279	4	21	187	82	46	516	197
South Bohemian Region	96	1,985	721	8	45	460	215	94	1,525	506
Olomouc Region	57	801	299	5	26	225	96	56	576	203
Zlín Region	46	494	187	7	34	268	107	45	226	80
Moravian-Silesian Region	120	1,973	723	9	72	665	304	119	1,308	419

Table 13. Education in full-time secondary schools – learners without disability and disabled learners in mainstream schools and special schools (Source: www.uiv.cz)

Type of education / Length of education	completion year – 7	completion year – 6	completion year – 5	completion year – 4	completion year – 3	completion year – 2	completion year – 1	completion year
Total	9,277	9,071	11,299	11,333	70,494	97,271	98,840	96,502
secondary education	0	0	0	0	0	0	926	1,443
2-year	0	0	0	0	0	0	926	863
1-year	0	0	0	0	0	0	0	580
secondary education with an apprenticeship certificate	0	0	0	0	0	30,621	28,000	27,364
3-year	0	0	0	0	0	30,621	26,963	26,549
2-year	0	0	0	0	0	0	1,037	815
general secondary education with a maturita exam	9,277	9,071	11,299	11,333	22,570	22,285	21,471	21,315
8-year	9,277	9,071	8,944	8,961	8,084	8,096	7,712	7,832
6-year	0	0	2,355	2,372	2,184	2,020	1,974	1,974
5-year	0	0	0	0	0	0	0	0
4-year	0	0	0	0	12,302	12,169	11,785	11,509
technical secondary education with a maturita exam	0	0	0	0	47,924	44,365	42,655	41,259
4-year	0	0	0	0	47,924	44,365	42,655	41,259
post-secondary study	0	0	0	0	0	0	5,732	4,013
2-year	0	0	0	0	0	0	5,732	4,013
shortened secondary study with an apprenticeship certificate	0	0	0	0	0	0	7	972

2-year	0	0	0	0	0	0	1	28
1.5-year	0	0	0	0	0	0	6	25
1-year	0	0	0	0	0	0	0	919
shortened secondary study with a maturita exam	0	0	0	0	0	0	49	136
2-year	0	0	0	0	0	0	49	20
1-year	0	0	0	0	0	0	0	116
secondary education for learners with SEN	0	0	0	0	140	1,202	2,065	2,493
secondary education	0	0	0	0	0	0	727	1,238
2-year	0	0	0	0	0	0	727	684
1-year	0	0	0	0	0	0	0	554
secondary education with an apprenticeship certificate	0	0	0	0	0	1,066	1,189	1,087
3-year	0	0	0	0	0	1,066	842	780
2-year	0	0	0	0	0	0	347	307
general secondary education with a maturita exam	0	0	0	0	5	17	0	10
4-year	0	0	0	0	5	17	0	10
technical secondary education with a maturita exam	0	0	0	0	135	119	117	136
4-year	0	0	0	0	135	119	117	136
post-secondary study	0	0	0	0	0	0	32	22
2-year	0	0	0	0	0	0	32	22

Table 14. Disabled learners in secondary schools in school years between 2006 and 2017 (according to the type of disability) (source: MŠMT database)

Type of disability		2006/07	2007/08	2008/09	2009/10	2010/11	2011/12	2012/13	2013/14	2014/15	2015/16	2016/17
Disabled and disadvantaged learners in total[1,2]		16,239	14,638	13,540	13,444	12,199	11,830	11,353	11,004	10,853	10,541	9,853
out of which	intellectually disabled	13,233	11,331	10,619	10,285	8,738	8,369	7,342	6,847	6,807	6,359	5,818
	hearing impaired	392	395	387	355	319	289	269	279	280	279	234
	sight impaired	289	271	223	148	158	150	131	148	138	166	138
	speech impaired[3]	12	11	17	18	28	42	52	44	58	62	54
	physically disabled	495	475	432	430	393	375	378	351	311	312	294
	with multiple disabilities	549	695	747	970	856	932	993	1,025	1,181	1,316	1,492
	with developmental learning disorders[3]	1,245	1,430	1,058	1,162	1,622	1,562	1,647	1,689	1,350	1,208	1,009
	with developmental behavioural disorders[3]	.	.	.	.	.	.	286	310	347	368	270
	with medically diagnosed autism	24	30	57	76	85	111	255	311	381	471	544

Girls only [1,2]	4,145	4,407	4,455	4,479	4,651	4,834	4,963	5,640	5,665	6,145	6,673
out of which intellectually disabled	2,600	2,815	2,929	2,912	3,121	3,537	3,691	4,410	4,516	4,788	5,413
hearing impaired	113	126	124	123	115	128	136	160	165	159	172
sight impaired	57	68	57	61	53	68	66	66	113	138	149
speech impaired [3]	19	14	18	16	22	16	11	12	12	5	4
physically disabled	120	125	130	151	160	150	150	154	174	194	200
with multiple disabilities	668	578	493	441	408	373	366	389	311	299	249
with developmental learning disorders [3]	383	440	491	598	608	543	526	430	361	553	482
with developmental behavioural disorders [3]	76	142	133	119	114	.	.	.	.	.	.
with medically diagnosed autism	109	99	80	58	50	19	17	19	13	9	4

Notes:

[1] Data only for full-time form of education.

[2] Special classes including classes at schools established for children with SEN.

[3] Since school year 2016/17, only learners with "severe speech impairment," "severe behavioural disorders," and "severe developmental learning disorders" have been monitored.

The data presented here lead to reflections on the improving tendency in the field of inclusive education in the Czech Republic. The Ministry of Education, Youth and Sports defines inclusive education and ensuring equal conditions in the access to education as one of its priorities, specified in the document "Strategy for Educational Policy of the Czech Republic until 2020." The aim of the educational policy is to significantly eliminate inequality in education through increasing the quality of the entire educational system. In order to achieve the above-mentioned global objective, the basic measures involve not only the establishment of formal conditions for the implementation of adequate legislation and finance, but also the establishment of a functional professional background for mainstream school teachers, so that the requirements for high-quality inclusive education can be fulfilled.

Support will be provided for the target group, including mainstream school teachers, children and students, as well as parents and other caregivers taking part in upbringing and education of learners with special educational needs.

Disabled learners from the perspective of classmates without disability

Introduction

At present, disability has become a social topic particularly in relation to inclusive education. Social attitudes towards otherness have been formed throughout history under the influence of philosophy, politics, religion, and awareness raising. Attitudes in the individual perspective of every member of the society have been created in a similar way. Thus, disability and the people affected by it have become an integral part of the society. In this context, the key concepts are the norm, normality, and difference – the otherness of individuals or groups. There is still a certain amount of tension between altruism and egoism. This seems to be reflected in the attitudes of fully abled individuals towards those who differ, in particular by their potential, performance, or ability to succeed in society. All participants of inclusive education are deeply affected by this relationship, regardless of their position, occupation or their relation with the disabled individual. An acceptable form of this relationship, being the final form of the individual perspective and the attitude towards the disabled, evolves with upbringing. Even loving parents, if their new-born baby turns out to be disabled, need time and energy to shape their relationship into a mutually acceptable, emotionally fulfilling and torment-free form. The same applies to learners without disability who become – mostly at their own choice – the classmates of those not belonging, from the angle of their medical condition, to the group of their "normal" peers.

In the role of a learner, the disabled child is in constant interaction with their social environment and may show manifestations of selflessness, sympathy, empathy, altruism, etc., as well as impose uncommon requirements on their environment (attracting attention, provocation, raising pity, etc.). An advantage of the school environment, compared to the family one, is that a professional, i.e. a teacher, may develop and cultivate positivity and "work on" the ideas and manifestations of negativity.

Attitudes and adolescents

The basis for further discussion is a definition by Hartl (2010), who defines an "attitude" as a tendency to react in a steady manner to objects, persons, situations and to oneself. In this definition, attitudes are a measurable part of a personality structure, reflecting tendencies, interests and the educational level. Within the theoretical background, one may define five groups of attitudes: *emotional, intellectual, action-oriented, symmetric,* and *ego-defensive.* Atkinson (Nolen-Hoeksema et al., 2012) described functions attributed to the attitudes. These are the instrumental function – attitudes of the utilitarian character; knowledge function – this function is involved in the general view of the world. The value function of an attitude reflects the individual's value orientation or value hierarchy. The ego-defensive function is characterized by the Freudian displacement of negative elements and by the defence or even hostility towards people bearing these elements.

Some trouble appears in measuring attitudes and processing the obtained data, as it was indicated by Vávra (2006). The author presented other definitions of attitudes and provided generalizing characteristics: "While it cannot be said that all definitions describe the same, there is a significant correspondence among them. Attitudes are relatively steady, learnt; in fact they are (emotional) evaluations of certain objects or acting, and they organize acting towards these objects. Some emphasize the relationship towards acting, while others (as mentioned below) reject such a direct relationship. Some emphasize the multi-component nature of the attitude – that it comprises evaluation, feelings as well as manners of acting towards the object of the particular attitude. There is no unambiguous delimitation of what an attitude is and if comparing several of them, the only thing one may gain is certain intuitive understanding. An attitude is a scientific construction which does not mean anything negative in itself but needs to be kept in mind."

Particular attitudes towards the phenomenon of disability were investigated by Giami et al. (2007). In their research they identified the lack of information and social awareness of disability as a social phenomenon.

Shakespeare and Watson (2001) investigated the concept of disabilities and the disabled in society from the biological and social perspectives. The concept of a disability as a medical problem may be encountered even in the Czech context. This tends to create social barriers and thus influences the extent to which the disabled are accepted.

Characterization of the target group

Adolescence is the age in which both the individual's personality and social skills become mature, as well as their application in practical life. This period of searching, finding, consolidation and loss located between childhood and adulthood is the time of developmental changes built on personal experience and the first attempts at constructing relationships on the basis of the known in combination with the emotional input. The age category of 17–20 years, which may be characterized as late adolescence (Macek, 1999), defines the target group selected for the research into attitudes towards disabled peers. Late adolescence brings into the individuals' lives a combination of their own personality, which is getting mature, and their reflections on the environment in which it takes place. It is obvious that this process is dynamic and without clearly determined temporal boundaries. Adolescents work with their own experiences and are able to rationalize and generalize them independently. This is the basis for the adolescent's capability to correct the area of interpersonal relationships after a mistake is identified and the correctness of the solution is evaluated. This learning process, however, contributes to the lack of emotional stability with regard to the good and bad. The uncertainty caused by the learning process may be reflected in an alternation of particular attitudes adopted towards people or phenomena.

Here, it is necessary to point to the role of experience, which – although not rationalized, contributes to the establishment of a relationship towards a phenomenon, person, community or society. This is considered important, as it may often fundamentally influence an individual in the above defined age category in their attitudes and even the subsequent behaviour. In relation to this age category, developmental psychology mentions attentional fluctuation which induces an increased number of inaccurate images of reality created by focusing on the unsubstantial and partial distancing from a complex perspective. Relationships and their assessments are closely interrelated with the capability of abstracting. Despite the increasing importance of the role of logical thinking and the above-mentioned abstraction, the emotional concept of social relationships and situations is affected by uncertainty and unsteadiness during decision making.

Apart from the emotional development, adolescents in this period try to involve a rationalized perspective based on acquired information. If the information is missing or its existence is not realized by the adolescent, social situations and relationships lead to uncertainty in their formation and preservation. This age category was selected for this study because, from the standpoint of developmental psychology, during this period the individual develops the potential for systematic thinking, logical reflections and operations in semantic fields. It may therefore be presumed that an adolescent is able to establish relations between concepts and subsequently create their own attitudes. Adolescents' emotional experience is full of searching, effort of self-expression and reflections of the demands imposed by the environment, leading to an increase in one's own prestige. This is closely related to the need of assessment – both assessment of the environment and self-assessment. All of the above-mentioned factors are driven by the goal to achieve the highest possible level of emancipation. In the area of social relationships, which are closely associated with the topic of the study, this means the capability to objectively view the environment and to search for values in interpersonal relationships with the added value of responsibility and pursuit of steadiness. A stable self-concept provides room for the adolescents' sense of empathy and effort to understand people in their close surroundings and to attribute their own values to a particular relationship. At the stage of planning the study, an assumption was formulated that the target group of adolescents would be able to relate their knowledge and reflections to the reality of people in their surroundings and to establish attitudes, relationships and patterns of behaviour towards these individuals.

Methodology of data collection and processing

In order to collect the data necessary for research on the attitudes of fully abled adolescents towards their disabled peers, a survey was created. After a pilot test, adjustments were made to the survey – its final form comprises inquiries about necessary demographic data, followed by twenty-four survey questions, both open and closed ones. The survey investigation was conducted by members of the research team with identical instructions. Participants filled out their surveys on the spot.

Research sample and its characterization

The research involved 769 learners of secondary schools, randomly selected within the territory of the Czech Republic. The sample of schools included those providing education ending with a *maturita* exam or an apprentice-ship certificate. The sample contained more girls – 457, compared to 311 boys. The demographic data also included the study year in the respective school. Here, the amount of participants was equal for the first to third year of study. There was a lower number of participants in their fourth year of study, as the statistics did not include learners in programmes completed with the *maturita* exam, who had already left schools (Table 15).

Table 15. Distribution of participants in the individual years of study

Year of study	Frequency	Percentage
1.0	244	31.7
2.0	182	23.7
3.0	220	28.6
4.0	123	16.0
Total	769	100.0

One of the issues monitored by the survey was the concept of health insurance. The aim was to get the respondents' own description of health insurance (the question did not require definitions). The answers were assessed with regard to their correlation to an expert definition, i.e. based on their understanding of the concept, regardless of the used wording or forms of personal expression. Approximately 77.9 % of learners did not manage to describe their health insurance.

To establish an attitude towards a particular group of people, an adolescent needs previous experience to be subsequently used when creating the relationship. The survey provided some data regarding experience with the individual types of disabilities reported by the learners. The percentages were as follows: sight impairment 40.8 %, hearing impairment 22.5 %, physical disability 40.8 %, mental disability 37.2 %, and other (not listed) 5 %. It is clear from the sum of the percentages listed above that in numerous cases participants reported experience with more than one form of disability. Subsequently, due attention was drawn to the frequency of encounters with the disabled. Personal experience with the issue in a family or close vicinity was declared by 142 participants, i.e. 18.5 %.

The survey entry "Conditions for disabled individuals are satisfactory in our country" monitored the participants' awareness of the issue. A range of opinions occurred here, from strong approval to strong disapproval of the statement. The group of participants who answered "I don't know" deserves further investigation: almost half of the students (47.1 %) do not feel sufficiently informed.

The survey also provided the data concerning assistance for disabled people. From the total amount of participants, 47.7 % realize they have been asked to provide such assistance. In 7 cases, the participants refused to provide assistance; 424 participants (53.8 %) mention helplessness in such a situation – they did not know how to fulfil a request for assistance.

The survey question "Have you ever participated in some course or training focused on assistance for people with various disabilities?" inquired about the source of information for the participants. Approximately one fifth (19.5 %) of the participants were acquainted with an area of assistance provided to the disabled at a course or a seminar focused especially on this issue.

Regardless of the particular type of disability, one of the best sources of experience and information is voluntary work or another form of collaboration with organizations working for or with disabled people. The field investigated in the research is not an exception. Only a very low number of participants (36, i.e. 4.7 %) reported personal experience in the field, often only episodic.

The participants were subsequently asked to express their opinion on the provision of information about the issue during their study in secondary school. The results show that 10.4 % of participants were satisfied, while 684 (88.9 %) participants considered the provided information insufficient (13.1 %), superficial (31.6 %) or completely missing (44.2 %).

The next question inquired whether the respondents had any negative experiences with the disabled. Affirmative answers included reports of aggression, harassment, indecent behaviour, hindering an activity, groping, too close contact from the disabled person, harming someone else, different behaviour, lack of consideration for one's environment, and the need to revise more at school. The majority of participants (90.6 %) did not report any negative experience.

The participants were asked to specify which type of disability they felt the greatest concern for in relation to communication with disabled people. They expected communication to be less difficult with persons with sight impairment and physical disability (295, i.e. 38.4 %), while more difficulty was expected in communication with people with speech or hearing impairment (474, i.e. 61.6 %).

The question "Do you think that students with any type of disability are significantly advantaged or favoured?" inquired about the attitude to possible adjustments in study conditions. As the results show, 624 participants (81.1 %) do not feel any such favouring.

In relation to the assessment of information provided during the study, which was regarded as insufficient by 684 participants (88.9 %), the answers concerning interest in others and additional and more thorough information about the disabled were investigated.

Another objective was the assessment of study conditions for disabled learners. The focus of the question was whether the participants felt that the school and study environment provided comparable conditions and opportunities for both learners with and without disability. Only 26.8 % of participants consider these conditions to be comparable, and 37.3 % of the participants chose the option "I don't know."

The next survey section was the following: "Do you feel uncomfortable in the presence of a disabled person?" A positive answer was given by 46 participants (6 %); 61.1 % of participants did not perceive the situation as problematic, and the remaining 31.3 % did not feel able to specify their feeling.

The participants were also asked about their potential willingness to provide assistance to a disabled classmate. This service was taken for granted by 41.9 %; another 45.6 % agreed while simultaneously expressing their uncertainty concerning the kind or form of help and their own competence. The answer of 11 % of participants was negative: they would either not help at all or rely on the help of a competent person, or they believe that such a student should be self-reliant.

The following section focused on the character of help and the options of assistance provided to a disabled learner. Similarly to some of the previous questions, the relevance of the answers was investigated in this question. The participants formed two groups of a very similar size (49.5 % and 50.5 %). The answers show an obvious difference in the awareness of the options of help.

The question "Can you imagine having a disabled classmate? Do you think that for some disabilities it would not be possible to learn together?" inquired about the real idea of a disabled classmate and the possibility of common education. One third of the participants had a positive attitude to the statement. The rest of participants (505, i.e. 65.7 %) either responded negatively, or stated they did not know. As indicated by the answers, there is room for further work at school in this area.

The last survey question was formulated as follows: "In your opinion, what should be changed about the approach towards disabled people?" From the answers provided by the participants, 46.2 % were relevant. The remaining participants (53.8 %) were not capable of evaluating the situation and providing a relevant answer.

Conclusions

- A definition of health insurance was not formed by 77.9 % of learners, who were not able to describe the phenomenon. The majority of respondents (approximately 75 %) have personal experience of an encounter with a disabled person.

- Almost half of the participants were not able to express their opinion on the living conditions of the disabled in the Czech Republic.
- There were 53.8 % of respondents who either refused to provide assistance or did not feel competent enough to help.
- 80.5 % of learners do not take advantage of the offer of extra-curricular education in the field of disabilities.
- 95.3 % of learners do not participate in extra-curricular activities focused on work for or with the disabled.
- Information provided at school and in classes is considered insufficient by 88.9 % of participants.
- The vast majority of participants (90.6 %) do not have any negative experience with the disabled.
- 38.4 % of participants incorrectly assessed the actual difficulty in communication with a disabled person.
- Potential adjustments to the environment needed for study of disabled learners are regarded as necessary by 81.1 % of the participants. However, the vast majority (88.9 %) consider their awareness and competences related to a potential disabled classmate unsatisfactory and are interested in gaining further information in this area.
- The study opportunities for all learners are described as incomparable by 73.2 % of the respondents.
- Only 6 % of respondents reported they feel uncomfortable when meeting disabled people.
- 45.6 % or participants reported not knowing how to assist a disabled classmate; the majority of them would like to help. In contrast, almost half of the respondents were not able to suggest a relevant form of help or assistance.
- For 65.7 % of respondents, an idea of having a disabled learner in their class educated together with them was unimaginable.
- 53.8 % of respondents failed to describe in a relevant way the changes and adjustments to the environment that may be necessary for the disabled.

Recommendations for school practice

Regarding the area of health insurance and its clients, it is necessary to increase awareness and possibly also the skills of secondary school learners without disabilities. The most suitable opportunity is to do this within curricular subjects. It is, however, not necessary to create monothematic lessons or include this area in teaching in an unsuitable way.

From the perspective of the psychological development of an individual during adolescence, this period offers the best opportunity to familiarize learners with options of voluntary work focused on activities with or for the disabled. At this age, learners are mentally, emotionally and physically mature, so such an activity may become fulfilling for them. In order to increase awareness and subtilize attitudes towards disabled people, it is highly beneficial to collaborate with organizations for the disabled or schools for learners with special educational needs. Such collaboration is mutually rewarding.

Sentiments, attitudes and concerns of teaching staff in regard to inclusive education

Introduction

Inclusive education brings the opportunity to fulfil the educational needs of disabled learners within mainstream schools. In order to implement this, a transformation of all parameters involved in the process is necessary. This change is not related only to schools, but to the complex material and social environments, including parents of children without disability, parents of learners accepting the inclusive form of education and also teaching staff and fully abled classmates. The basic framework of inclusive education is established by an exact definition. However, it is modified in the individual national contexts and formed according to the social attitudes, and economic and cultural potentialities. The general objective of the study was to identify and characterize the conditions leading to an improvement in the policy and professional training of teaching staff for such a specific occupation as inclusive education. This occupation does not involve only didactic and methodological knowledge, but also the skills of teaching staff related to work with the other above mentioned participants of this complex process.

A key role in the process of inclusive education is played by the teaching staff. The level of acceptance, understanding and adoption of values concerning inclusive education on the part of teachers directly influences the quality of the adaptation of learners with disability and those without it, who are a creative component of the social climate in a group of children.

What may be perceived as an outcome of a harmonious interconnection is the fulfilled educational level and successful implementation of the formative component. A very effective supportive element, if it is present at a sufficient level, is motivation – the motivation of the teaching staff, who are able to spread their own motivation and pass it down to learners.

Another important factor in acquiring knowledge concerning the profession of a teacher in inclusive education is the effort to create the profile of a teacher, the requirements concerning professional skills, categories of attitudes, concerns and experiences in the possibly largest variety. Such characteristics enable not only the field work of advisors, but also a specific focus on particular problems related to the training of future teachers. As numerous scholars point out, even short-term courses or instructional trainings may lead to change, especially in the category of teachers' attitudes towards inclusive education, and thus – may help to overcome the barriers to more efficient motivation for such work (Shade, Stewart, 2001). The previous studies are based on the finding that teachers' attitudes towards inclusion are often not grounded in ideological or political beliefs, but instead in practical concerns about how to implement inclusive education and fulfil the requirements imposed on them in general (Burke, Sutherland, 2004; Scruggs, Mastropieri, 1996).

With regard to this, the study focuses on the analysis of attitudes and self-reflection of teachers who work in mainstream schools, have no professional training in special pedagogy, but potentially may, nevertheless, play an important role in inclusive education.

Methodology of data collection and processing

The data collection was conducted with the use of the SACIE-R survey, the latest version of the tool published in 2011 (Forlin et al., 2011). The basis for the latest, reduced version was the original SACIE survey (Loreman et al., 2007), created within the international research project SACIE (Sentiments, Attitudes & Concerns about Inclusive Education). The international research team consisted of Ch. Forlin – Institute of Education Hong Kong; T. Loreman and Ch. Earle – Concordia University College of Alberta, Canada; and U. Sharma, Monash University, Victoria, Australia. The study was focused on the sentiments, attitudes and concerns of teaching staff when dealing with the disabled. The shortened version was verified by the authors in a practical study and was assessed as functional (Forlin et al., 2011), An adjustment of this tool was done in accordance with the common method of translation and back translation, which verified the content correspondence of the individual components with the original. The SACIE-R survey consists of fifteen questions formulated in the way which enables the subsequent analysis and characterization of the three categories – sentiments, attitudes, and concerns – which are significantly involved in the professional relationship, work efficiency and motivation of teachers working in the environments of inclusive education. In compliance with the ethical requirements of pedagogical research and reflecting the ethic code APA (APA, 2010), all data was collected upon the participants' informed consent and complete anonymity was maintained in relation to both the respondents and their workplaces.

The survey was conducted in paper/pencil format from May to November 2018. Filled out questionnaires expanded to include demographic data were continuously transferred into a Microsoft Excel document and subsequently to the programme IBM SPSS 21, where the data analysis was performed. The first step was descriptive statistics, followed by factor analysis. In order to determine correlations among the factors, Pearson's correlation coefficient was used.

The research sample and its composition

The request for collaboration was addressed directly to the teaching staff in the following regions: Olomouc, South Bohemia, Plzeň, North Bohemia, Hradec Králové, South Moravia, North Moravia, Liberec and the Capital City of Prague. In all cases, the participants were active teachers at preschool, primary or secondary education levels. An obligatory condition was the exclusion of teachers who had completed or were studying special pedagogy while working at mainstream school facilities. The sample group consisted of 780 respondents (N=780).

Analysis and processing of research data

The 780 filled questionnaires (N=780) were used in the further data processing. As the first step, the processing involved descriptive statistics of the demographic data and an analysis of answers to questions about experience, awareness and education in relation to the issue of the disabled. Out of the total number of participants, there were 54 men and 721 women; 5 participants did not provide information regarding their sex.

The research sample in the study corresponds to the distribution of respondents in the original sample (Forlin et al., 2011). It also corresponds to the average data for the Czech Republic regarding the presence of men and women in the educational sector. According to the annual statistical survey of the Ministry of Education, Youth and Sports, the total number of primary school teachers in 2016/2017 is 73,405. Out of this number, there are 61,478 women (i.e. 83.75 %).

Age of respondents

The participants were divided into three categories based on their age: up to 29 years – 235 participants; 30–39 years – 222 participants; 40 years and more – 320 participants. 3 respondents did not provide the information. The sample of participants may be considered balanced as regards the representation of the above defined age categories.

Education of respondents

Half of the participants (51 %) reported that they had finished secondary education but were studying at university at that time. The remaining 48 % had completed university education (either Bachelor's or Master's degree). There were 1 % of participants who did not provide any information about completed education. Neither the ongoing university studies nor the completed ones were focused on special pedagogy; they usually involved the acquisition of teaching qualification for selected subjects or the study aimed at an extension of the portfolio of subject qualifications or new qualifications.

Respondents' occupation

The majority of participants were teachers at mainstream primary schools and mainstream nursery schools. Therefore, these respondents did not choose to work mostly with disabled children. The sample included a group of participants characterized as "outside the education sector." They were primarily women on maternity leave. A minority of participants reported work in special school; these participants, however, did not report

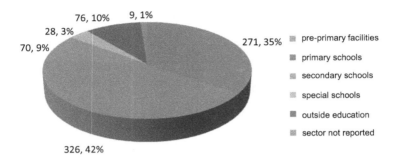

Figure 5. The percentage distribution of respondents' workplaces

any previous education in special pedagogy or present study in this field (Figure 5).

Contact with disabled people

The majority of participants (60 %) state that they have not been in contact with disabled persons yet, which is considered important particularly from the perspective of the monitored parameters for the formation of fundamental concepts of health insurance, its clients, and relationships created by this fact (Table 16).

The perception of respondents' professional readiness

The lack of readiness for work with disabled learners was reported by 42 % of participants and insufficient readiness by 33 %. Summing up, there are 75 % of active teachers who do not feel sufficiently equipped for pedagogical work in the inclusive environment. In contrast, 23 % of participants feel sufficiently equipped. The remaining part consists of participants who did not provide any assessment (Table 17).

Table 16. Numerical expression of respondents' contact with the disabled

Contact with a disabled person	Abs. frequency
yes	306
no	469
not reported	5

Table 17. Self-assessment of respondents' readiness for work with disabled learners

Professional readiness	Abs. frequency
lacking	330
insufficient	260
sufficient	175
not indicated	15

Awareness of the legislative background concerning the upbringing and education of disabled learners

Only 23 % of the participants considered their awareness of the legislative framework for inclusive education to be very good or good. With regard to the subjectivity of assessment, this may be considered sufficient for the performance of pedagogical work in the conditions of inclusive education. Apart from the 1 % of participants who did not answer, there are again around 75 % of the participants who regarded the information they have about this area as insufficient.

Confidence in educating disabled learners

The assessment of "confidence in educating disabled learners" was very similar as in the previous section. It was assessed as good or very good by 23 % of participants; 2 % did not answer, and the remaining 75 % did not feel confident to perform such work (Table 18).

Table 18. Respondents' confidence in work with disabled learners

Confidence rate	Abs. frequency
very good	32
good	149
average	269
low	176
rather unsure	135
not indicated	19

Perception of experience with education of disabled learners

The experience was considered sufficient for inclusive education by 20 % of participants. Apart from the 3 % of those who did not answer, 77 % of participants did not possess experience in the education of disabled learners (Table 19).

Awareness of the opportunities to get professional help

The majority of participants (73 %) state that their awareness of opportunities to ask for professional help if they should educate a disabled learner is sufficient. They know about the options of consulting, advice and help available to them. The remaining 26 % are not informed.

Statistical analysis of the collected data

Further processing of the data involved factor analysis, which enabled verification of the validity of scales in the adapted form of survey for the Czech population.

Factor Analysis

First of all, it was investigated whether the data is suitable for factor analysis (the value of KMO =,771, sig.,000). Both values indicate the suitability of the data for factor analysis. The anti-image matrix was created as well, in which the values of MSA exceeded 0.5 in all cases (they were situated within the range of 0.64 – 0.88). The values of communality lay in the range of 0.4 – 0.8, apart from one item, of which the value was 0.3. The suitability for factor analysis was confirmed by this again.

Table 19. Respondents' own experience with the education of the disabled

Experience	Abs. frequency
insufficient	352
little	252
sufficient	156
not indicated	20

In accordance with the Kaiser criterion, the selected factors were those with the "eigenvalue" exceeding 1.0. There were four such factors, accounting for almost 60 % of variance in the items. To enable better interpretation, the varimax rotation method was used. Factor loadings range from 0.5 to 0.9. The above-mentioned factors, except for the first one, correspond to the individual scales of the survey, as set by the authors of the tool (Forlin et al., 2011). In the case of the first one, for the category of "sentiments" the factor is split into two sub-categories: "sentiments A 1–3" and "sentiments B 4–5." Categories "attitudes" (6–1) and "concerns" (11–15). Subsequently, correlation factor analysis was conducted in the programme IBM SPSS AMOS. This analysis confirmed that the factor "concern" splits into two factors in the case of this sample.

Correlation of scales with variables

The obtained factors were later correlated with each other and with the individual variables based on the demographic data (age, sex, confidence, experience, etc.).

Sources influencing participants' opinions, concerns and attitudes

The analysis revealed correlations at the 0.01 significance level, but their strength was not significant. For further interpretation, correlation values between 0.3–0.49 were accounted for. According to De Vaus (De Vaus, 2001), they are regarded as moderate to substantial, and the correlation values in the range of 0.5–0.69 may be considered substantial to very strong.

The relationship between the factor "sentiments A" and the factor "concerns":

• Participants agreeing with the third factor tended to disagree with the second factor (i.e. they agreed being concerned about the presence of disabled learners and rather disagreed to these children being educated at mainstream schools).

Contact with disabled persons and expertise, awareness, confidence, and experience

• Participants who have not encountered any disabled people (60 %) feel:

  – rather unprepared professionally,

– rather insufficiently informed,
– rather uncertain, and
– do not have experience.

Expertise and awareness, confidence, and experience

• Participants who have assessed themselves as not being professionally prepared to a sufficient extent for work with disabled children and learners (42 %, and 75 %), report:

– having too little information,
– not feeling confident, and
– not having sufficient experience.

Awareness and confidence, experience, and the ability to gain information

• Participants who have reported not having information on the legislative framework (35 %):

– feel rather uncertain,
– have insufficient experience, and
– do not know where to ask.

Confidence and experience, awareness of sources of information and support

• Participants feeling rather uncertain (41 %) simultaneously:

– have insufficient experience, and
– do not know where to ask.

Experience and awareness of the sources of information and support

• Participants who have assessed their experience as insufficient (45 %, and 77 %) simultaneously reported not knowing where to ask for advice, consulting or professional help.

The common feature in this characterization of the respondents is the fact that they did not choose to work with disabled children, do not have knowledge and experience, and at the same time show the highest level of concern (Table 20).

The table above clearly indicates that the participants answered in a very similar way. This may be the reason why it was impossible to prove

Table 20. The most frequent answers to individual questions in the applied questionnaire

Question	Answer	Percentage
1. It is hard to overcome the initial shock when meeting people with severe disability.	disagree	53 %
2. I am afraid of direct contact with disabled people.	disagree	57 %
3. I try to establish only a brief contact with disabled people and to end it quickly.	disagree	61 %
4. I would feel terrible if I were disabled.	agree	56 %
5. I am scared of the thought that I might become disabled.	agree	47 %
6. Learners who have difficulty with verbal expressing their thoughts should be taught in mainstream classes.	agree / disagree	40 % / 46 %
7. Learners with continuously unsatisfactory results belong to mainstream classes.	disagree	64 %
8. Learners educated according to an individual education plan should be in mainstream classes.	agree	60 %
9. Learners with attention deficit belong to mainstream classes.	agree / disagree	54 % / 36 %
10. Learners in need of special communication techniques (Braille, sign language) for their education belong to mainstream classes.	disagree	57 %
11. I believe that the presence of a disabled learner would significantly increase my workload.	agree	58 %
12. I am afraid that it would be difficult to pay appropriate attention to all learners (including the disabled) in a mainstream class.	strongly agree / agree	42 % / 48 %
13. I am afraid that the presence of a disabled learner would be a source of large mental burden.	agree / disagree	48 % / 31 %
14. I am afraid that disabled learners would not be well-accepted in classes of not disabled peers.	agree / disagree	39 % / 44 %
15. I am afraid that my readiness for work with disabled learners is not sufficient to achieve the necessary results.	agree	54 %

the difference in relation to their age, length of practice, education, and gender. The level of opinions is the same or very similar in most cases.

Conclusion

The statistical processing of the data and the subsequent analysis involved 780 filled questionnaires with the use of the Czech version of SACIE-R.

The descriptive statistics have shown that:

- out of the total number of 780 respondents, 92 % were women;
- the age distribution of the participants in the three categories up to 29 years, 30–39 years, and 40 and more years was balanced and there was no necessity to take into account the influence of age on the results;
- for the majority of participants, their completed education was at the secondary level (51 %), the Bachelor's degree (17 %) and the Master's degree (31 %);
- 86 % of participants reported an occupation outside special pedagogy;
- 60 % of participants have not experienced contact with a disabled person;
- 75 % of participants characterize their professional readiness for work in inclusive environments as lacking or insufficient;
- 65 % of participants assess their orientation in the field of legislation focused on inclusive education as very good to average;
- 75 % of participants assess their feeling of confidence in education of disabled learners as unsatisfactory;
- 77 % of participants realize the absence of experience in pedagogical practice of inclusive education;
- 73 % of participants report being informed about possible sources of professional help or consulting.

Factor Analysis

The correlation of the obtained factors with variables of the demographic data revealed the following:

- the respondents are concerned about the presence of disabled learners and rather disagree to these children being educated at mainstream schools;

– those participants who have not experienced any contact with disabled individuals (60 %) feel that they are not professionally prepared, not sufficiently informed, and rather uncertain. Moreover, they feel that they do not have experience in pedagogical work with the target group in the inclusive environment;
– those respondents who assessed their own professional readiness for work with disabled learners as insufficient simultaneously report having little information, feeling uncertain and not having sufficient experience;
– those participants who reported not having sufficient information about the legislation of inclusive education feel rather uncertain, do not have sufficient experience and do not know the sources of information and options of consulting and professional help;
– those participants who feel rather uncertain simultaneously realize the lack of experience and also do not know the sources of professional help and consulting;
– those participants who assessed their own experience as insufficient also reported not knowing where to ask for advice, consulting or professional help.

The common feature in the above listed overview of the participants is the fact that they did not choose to perform pedagogical work in an inclusive environment, and that they realize their insufficient awareness and readiness, which is the reason for their higher level of concern and uncertainty. The presented results reveal space for possible interventions not only in relation to the teaching staff active in the discussed field, but also those who aim at the training of future teachers, as there seems to be a promising potential for the inclusive school environment.

Inclusive education in the Czech Republic: conclusions

The information presented above clearly confirms that inclusive education has started its journey within the educational system. While it is not a revolutionary innovation – disabled children have always been participants in the education mainstream, more attention from the state, society and even politicians have only been granted to this educational concept in the last years (since around 2016). As the speed of development of inclusive education has not been followed by the establishment of precise terminology, one may often encounter ambiguity as regards terms such as integration, inclusion or segregation even in the environment of professionals. The need for a higher level of acceptance of the promoted pedagogical concept has led to the term "common education." For practical use, integration may be understood as a process, while inclusion may be regarded as the person's attitude. Integration shall ensure the necessary compensatory aids and efficient teaching methods to reduce the impact of the learners' disability and thus enable the student to achieve their best possible performance at school. The concept of integration helps the child to fit in with the classmates.

Inclusive education is based on the premise that the integration is not only in the interest of the child who is being integrated, but in the interest of all participants. A prerequisite for successful inclusion is, however, a high level of tolerance and understanding. On the other hand, it is necessary to realistically assess every individual case, as inclusive education cannot be implemented in all cases. There are cases where children suffer from a severe disability or a combination of disabilities, and therefore their integration into the educational mainstream is not possible.

In conclusion to this chapter, having summarized the current state of inclusive education in the Czech Republic and supplemented it with the results of the study, it is possible to consider the following factors influencing the quality of inclusive education, its results and subsequently also the attitudes of the society. *The atmosphere at the school and attitudes towards inclusive education*: this factor concerns the preparation and determination of the social climate not only in a particular class, but at the entire school. The idea of inclusive education has to be accepted by the teachers, learners, parents as well as other school employees. Apart from physical accessibility, this also involves the availability of extra-curricular activities for learners. Classmates play an important part in the school performance and personal comfort of a child educated in the inclusive environment, so they should be prepared not only emotionally, but also in the field of the necessary social and technical skills, as these subsequently facilitate a mutually positive relationship. Another important area is the *methodical and didactic* work of the teacher. As demonstrated earlier, this aspect is regarded as the fundamental element of teachers' competences, if perceived by them as sufficient. On the contrary, its absence negatively influences not only the teachers' motivation, but also the general attitude towards inclusive education as a pedagogical phenomenon in the broadest context. This area also involves the organizational management of teaching, influenced to some extent by the presence of a teaching assistant, as well as the application of suitable forms and methods or work – under normal circumstances, these make the teaching efficient and motivating, in the case of inclusive education they shall ensure the same effect. The study presents teachers' attitudes and concerns, as well as the information about areas and topics threatening, to a certain extent, the successful work of teachers in the specific conditions of inclusive education.

References

American Psychological Association. (2010). Ethical principles of psychologists and code of conduct (2002, Amended June 1, 2010).

Antonínová, H., Nolen-Hoeksema, S. (2012). *Psychologie Atkinsonové a Hilgarda*. Praha: Portál.

Barrow, R., Woods, R. G. (2006). An introduction to philosophy of education. London: Routledge.

Bjarnason, D. S. (2005). Disability studies and their importance for special education professionals. *Nordisk Pedagogik*, 25(4), 339–356.

Brue, A.W., Wilmshurst, l. (2005). *A Parent´s Guide to Special Education*. New York: AMACOM.

Burke, K., Sutherland, C. (2004). Attitudes Toward Inclusion: Knowledge vs. Experience. *Education*, 125(2), 163–172.

Chlup, O. (1965). Pedagogika: Příručka pro vysoké školy (2. přepr. vyd. ed.). Praha: Státní pedagogické nakladatelství.

De Vaus, D. A. (2001). Research design in social research. London: SAGE.

Flynn, R. J., Lemay, R. (1999). A Quarter-Century of Normalization and Social Role Valorization: Evolution and Impact. Ottawa: University of Ottawa Press. Retrieved July 13, 2018, from Project MUSE database.

Forlin, C. (2006). Inclusive Education in Australia ten years after Salamanca. *European Journal of Psychology of Education,* 21(3), 265–277.

Forlin, C., Earle, C., Loreman, T., Sharma, U. (2011). The Sentiments, Attitudes, and Concerns about Inclusive Education Revised (SACIE-R)

Scale for Measuring Pre-Service Teachers' Perceptions about Inclusion. *Exceptionality Education International*, 21(3), 50–65.

Hájková, V. (2005). *Integrativní pedagogika*. Praha: IPPP ČR.

Hartl, P., Hartlová, H. (2010). *Velký psychologický slovník*. Praha: Portál, 2010.

Hull, K., Goldhaber, J., Capone, A. (2002). *Opening doors*. Boston: Houhgton Miffin Comp.

Jean-Louis, K., Lavigne, C., Giami, A. (2007). Representations, Metaphors and meaning of the Term Handicap in France: Representations of Handicap in France.

Jesenský, J. (1990). *Integrace – znamení doby*. Praha: Karolinum.

Jesenský, J. (1995). *Kontrapunkty integrace zdravotně postižených*. Praha: Karolinum.

Jílek, D., Větrovský, J., Migová, K. (2015). Segregace, vzdělávací příležitost a závazky států (1. vyd. ed.). Praha: Wolters Kluwer.

Jůva, V. (2001). Základy pedagogiky pro doplňující pedagogické studium. Brno: Paido.

Kocurová, M. et al. (2002). *Speciální pedagogika pro pomáhající profese*. Plzeň: ZČU.

Kolář, Z. et al. (2012). Výkladový slovník z pedagogiky: 583 vybraných hesel (Vyd. 1. ed.). Praha: Grada.

Loreman, T., Earle, Ch., Sharma, U., Forlin, Ch. (2007). The Development of an Instrument for Measuring Pre-service Teachers' Sentiments, Attitudes, and Concerns about Inclusive Education. *International Journal of Special Education*, 22 (2), 150–159.

Macek, P. (1999). *Adolescence: psychologické a sociální charakteristiky dospívajících*. Praha: Portál.

Machonin, P., Gatnar, L., Tuček, M. (2000). Vývoj sociální struktury v české společnosti. Sociologický ústav AV ČR, Praha.

Nolen-Hoeksema, S. et al., (2012) Psychologie Atkinsonové a Hilgarda. Vyd. 3., přeprac. Praha: Portál.

Potměšil, M. (2007). *Sebereflexe a sluchové postižení*. Praha: UK Praha, Karolinum.

Potměšil, M. et al. (2015). Speciálněpedagogická intervence u dětí v raném věku (1. vydání. ed.). Olomouc: Univerzita Palackého v Olomouci.

Průcha, J. (2001). Alternativní školy a inovace ve vzdělání. Praha: Portál.

Průcha, J. (2013). Moderní pedagogika (5., aktualiz. a dopl. vyd. ed.). Praha: Portál.

Průcha, J., Mareš, J., Walterová, E. (2013). Pedagogický slovník. Praha: Portál.

Puldová, P. (2011). Vzdělanostní struktura. In: M. Ouředníček, J. Temelová, L. Pospíšilová, (Eds.). Atlas sociálně prostorové diferenciace České republiky. Praha: Karolinum.

Scruggs, T. E., Mastropieri, M. A. (1996). Teacher perceptions of mainstreaming/inclusion, 1958–1995: A research synthesis. Exceptional Children, 63(1), 59–74.

Shade, R. A., Stewart, R. (2001). General Education and Special Education Preservice Teachers' Attitudes Toward Inclusion. Preventing School Failure, 46(1), 37–41.

Shakespeare, T., Watson, N. (2001). The social model of disability: An outdated ideology? JAI Press.

Sovák, M. (1980). Nárys speciální pedagogiky. 4. vyd. Praha: SPN.

Statistická ročenka školství 2016/2017 – Praha: Ústav pro informace ve vzdělávání výkonové ukazatele: C1.11. Základní vzdělávání – učitelé (počet, přepočtení na plně zaměstnané).

Vališová, A., Kasíková, H. (2011). Pedagogika pro učitele (2., rozš. a aktualiz. vyd. ed.). Praha: Grada.

Vávra, M. (2006). "Nesnáze s měřením postojů." SDA Info VIII (1), 9–12.

Legal documents

Zákon č. 561/2004 Sb., o předškolním, základním, středním, vyšším odborném a jiném vzdělávání, školský zákon. (2017). Praha: Tiskárna Ministerstva vnitra.

27/2016 Sb. o vzdělávání žáků se speciálními vzdělávacími potřebami a žáků nadaných, ve znění účinném od 1. 1. 2018.

72/2005 Sb. Vyhláška o poskytování poradenských služeb ve školství a školských poradenských zařízeních.

Ling Guo

Chapter 4 Inclusive education of learners with disability in China

Introduction

As a widely recognized concept of education and worldwide trend for the development of special education, inclusive education has been implemented in various forms in different countries. In China, inclusion has been understood at different levels, which can lead to different forms of inclusive education. Inclusive education has been practiced in the form of Learning in Regular Classroom (in the short form of LRC) based on China's unique social background and cultural determinants.

LRC has been regarded as a pragmatic way for implementing inclusive education based on the combination of the core spirit of inclusive education and the reality of Chinese society, which is more focused on increasing admission rate of children with disabilities into compulsory education than education for all. LRC is organized in general school under the professional guidance from special education resource centre supported by professional personnel and facilities of special education school. The implementation of LRC in China takes the top-down mode which largely depends on policy guarantee and financial support from the government.

After 30 years' development, the implementation of LRC has accomplished great success in increasing nationwide school admission and has become the main approach for developing special education as it provides education for the majority of children with disabilities in China. However, the quality of LRC has not been satisfying because of several barriers including the exam-oriented value of education, contradictory attitude to inclusive education, imperfect government policies, lack of funding guarantee and shortage of qualified teachers. In the future, LRC in China will be more focused on improving the quality of education for children with disabilities. The realization of this goal depends on the construction of a comprehensive supporting system for LRC, which covers a change of concept, improvement of policies and mechanism, the funding guarantee, improvement of teachers' qualifications, support from special school and special education resource centres.

4.1. Theoretical foundations of inclusive education

China, with the official name The People's Republic of China (PRC in short), is the third biggest country in the world with the area of more than 9.6 million square kilometres and the biggest population of 1.39 billion till the end of 2017 in the mainland (National Statistics Bureau of PRC, 2017). PRC was founded on October 1st, 1949, on the basis of the civilization more than 5 000 years old, and Beijing was chosen to be the capital of the whole country because of its important role in the history.

Under the leadership of the Communist Party of China, the central government of China executes jurisdiction in over 22 provinces, 5 autonomous minority regions (Tibet, Xinjiang, Ningxia, Inner Mongolia, and Guangxi), 4 municipalities (Beijing, Tianjin, Shanghai, Chongqing), and 2 special administrative regions of Hongkong and Macau. At the same time, as Taiwan has been an inseparable part of the Chinese nation since ancient times, the Chinese government also claims sovereignty over it. Because of historical reasons, a different political system has been implemented in Hongkong, Macau, and Taiwan if compared to the mainland of China. Correspondingly, the social conditions, economic level and educational development are also different. Given the large differences among special education among the three parts and mainland China, the inclusive education based on Chinese experience in this chapter is limited to the situation in mainland China.

4.1.1. Historical outline of education for disabled learners in China

Historical background of education for learners with disabilities

The development of special education, as an important indicator of social civilization and developmental level of a country, is always based on social stability, economic development and policy support. Hence, the development of special education is always consistent with certain stage of social development.

As one of the four ancient civilizations of the world, China has experienced a long history which can be divided into three stages: ancient, modern and contemporary times. The ancient time of Chinese history started from Xia. The first hereditary dynasty recorded in Chinese history books started around the 21st century BC and ended at the beginning of the Opium War in 1840. For millennia during this time, China expanded, fractured and re-unified numerous times, but the political system was always based on hereditary monarchies. In 221 BC, Qin unified six countries and built the first unified empire. Since then, China had started the history of feudal society till the middle of the 19th century. During this time, China experienced frequent replacement of dynasties and also developed a highly prosperous feudal civilization which affected many neighbouring countries and was known in some far west countries. This prosperous feudal civilization provided a good social environment for the sprout of special education in Chinese ancient history.

The modern times of Chinese history started in 1840 with the beginning of Opium War and ended in 1949, the establishment of PRC. During this time, China was invaded by western powers, due to the situation that their industrial civilization far exceeded the developmental level of China's agricultural civilization. Chinese government was forced to cede territories, pay indemnities and open ports for foreign trade. Along with opium and others western goods the western religion came as well as missionaries, who had important influence on the development of special education in modern China (Zhang, Ma, Du, 2000, pp. 196–197).

Since October 1st 1949, China started the contemporary history with the establishment of PRC. The new born Chinese government started to carry out large-scale socialist construction to let the country recover from the continuous war for about twenty years. After experiencing ten years stagnation in economic advancement, huge losses for both the whole country and individuals, and the havoc of social life during Cultural Revolution, the Reform and Opening up Policy were implemented in mainland China in 1978. After nearly 40 years of development, China has become one of the countries with the fastest-growing economy in the world and has jumped to be the world's second-largest economy according to GDP. In contemporary China, the rapid development in economy has promoted the advancement of special education, along with technological progress and enhancement of human self-awareness.

Corresponding stages of education for learners with disabilities

Similarly to the development of special education in the world, China has a long history of practical activities in special education, but a short history of it as a specialized discipline. Corresponding to the stages of its social background, the special education in China has also undergone the following three phases: preparation, formation, and vigorous growth (Mu, 2006, p. 37).

The preparation phase: the sprout of ancient thought about special education

In Chinese ancient literature, there were long records concerning persons with disabilities and the causes of these disabilities. For example, volume six of "Zuo Zhuan" says: "Ěr bù tīng wǔ shēng zhī hé wèi lóng, mù bù bié wǔ sè zhī zhāng wèi mèi," which means "people whose ear cannot hear sounds are deaf and people whose eyes cannot tell colours are blind." There were many words used to represent disabilities, including "Máng," "Gǔ," "Méng," "Sǒu" (blind), "Lóng," "kuì" (deaf), "Yīn yǎ" (speech disorder), "Qué," "bǒ," "Gōulóu" (physical disability), "Chī," "Dāi," "yú" (intellectual disability), "Fēng," "Diān" (mental disability), and the like (Huang, 2015). Besides this, there were also lots of records about extraordinary children in ancient literature. These records show that people gained basic knowledge of disabilities in ancient times, which have helped to give due human care to people with disabilities.

Although in ancient China there were also superstitious ideas about disabilities, which attributed disability to demon possession or retribution, in general, people with disabilities were treated with compassion and tolerance due to government's preferential treatment policy or government-funded care system. For example, as early as in the Xia Shang and Zhou Dynasties – more than 2000 years ago, there was a tax relief policy to people with disabilities and special institutions have been established to provide relief to disabled people since Sui dynasty around 1500 years ago (Zhang, Ma, Du, 2000, pp. 200–202). This tradition was continued by many subsequent dynasties to show the governor's kindness and improve the life situation of the disabled.

In ancient China, besides receiving a governmental relief, people with disabilities could also sometimes have access to education. According to the research, public education for disabled people took place in Zhou dynasty, which originated from the occupational skills training for blind musicians during Xia, Shang, Zhou dynasties (Mu, 2006, p. 38). Unfortunately, during the long feudal society for more than two thousand years, it was not possible for people with disabilities to go to educational institutions owned by the government and public special school did not exist at that time. In brief, people with disabilities were excluded from the educational system most of the time in ancient China. However, the awareness of disabilities and kind treatment of people with disabilities, along with the early attempts of skills training, laid a foundation for the emergence of modern special education.

The formation phase: the emergence of modern special education schools

With the first Opium War in 1840, China started to be a semi-colonial and semi-feudal society with social instability and struggling national education. During this time, special education in China mostly depended on missionaries from western countries. From the end of the Qing Dynasty to the beginning of the 20th century, on the one hand – missionaries in China wrote articles to introduce special education ideas and practices in western countries to China, and on the other hand, they personally founded some special education institutions in different places of China. For example, in 1874 a Scottish missionary William Murray built "Gǔ sǒu tōng wén guǎn" in Beijing which is now called Beijing School for the Blind. In 1887, an American missionary Mills built "Qǐ yīn xué guǎn" in Dengzhou in Shandong province, now called Yantai Speical Education School (Zhang, Ma, Du, 2000, p. 209). These two schools are recorded as the first special schools for the blind children and children with hearing impairment in China. Besides these two, there were some other special schools built by missionaries for children with hearing or visual impairment in other places of China, including Hankou, Tainan, Guangzhou, Fuzhou, and others.

These schools built by missionaries not only provided disabled children with educational opportunities, but also promoted people's early understanding and acceptance of special education in China, which further gave birth to the emergence of China's local special education schools. At the beginning of the 20ᵗʰ century, Liu Xianji, Zhang Jian, and Zhou Yuexian started to set up private special education schools (Mu, 2006, p. 38).

In 1921, the primary school attached to the Third Teachers' College in Jiangsu Province opened special class for children with intellectual disabilities, which was the first time when children with disabilities were accepted by public primary school and which started a new era in the development of special education in China (Gan, 2012, p. 26). On October 3ʳᵈ, 1927, School for Blind and Dumb Children was built in Nanjing. As the first public special education school in the modern times of China, its birth symbolized the government's direct participation in special education. Before the founding of PRC, there were 42 special schools for children with hearing or visual impairment, in which 2380 students were educated (Gu, 2001, p. 65). Yet, during that time, the recognized types of disabled students were restricted to children with deafness or blindness and most of these schools were private, which means that special education was thought as one part of social charities and the government participation was limited.

The vigorous growth phase: the establishment of modern special education system

In 1949, with the end of the Anti-Japanese War and the Civil War, the new country was built in China. After the foundation of PRC, the Chinese government promulgated the "Decision on the Reform of the Educational System." In this document, special education schools were prescribed to be set up for children with deafness or blindness, which symbolized that special education was firstly counted as one part of national education system (Zhao, Meng, 2008, p. 35). From that time on, the modern special education system has been gradually established in China.

From the foundation of PRC to the mid-1980s, special education school were always the main form of implementation of special education in mainland China. In the 1950s, the Ministry of Education issued several regulations to specify the funding, school organization, and so on, in special schools for deaf or blind children. The government also implemented the unified sign language in schools and workplaces for the deaf during that time. From the 1960s to the late 1970s, the special education in China was almost in a standstill because of the devastating Cultural Revolution for ten years.

Since 1978, on the one hand, along with the order of social life which was restored after Cultural Revolution, there was a rapid development in the construction of legal system for special education and a series of laws, regulations and documents related to special education were issued in succession. China's special education gradually embarked on the path compliant with the law. At the same time, however, along with the comparatively stable and open social environment after the Reform and Opening Policy, more experience of special education from foreign countries was introduced to China and the practice of special education aimed at meeting the actual educational needs of children with disabilities was attempted in China (Zhao, Meng, 2008, pp. 35–36).

From 1954 to the beginning of the Cultural Revolution, foreign students who came back from the former Soviet Union conducted educational experiment for children with intellectual disabilities. In 1979, the first special education class for children with intellectual disabilities was opened in Beijing and the first batch of Chinese special schools for intellectually disabled learners started to be established in 1983.

In 1987, China conducted the first national sample survey of disabled persons. The statistics showed that there were about 6.25 million children with disabilities at the school age range of compulsory education from 6 to 14 years. However, at that time, the enrolment rate of school-aged students with blindness or deafness was smaller than 6 %, which means that more than 5.87 million school-aged children with disabilities were excluded from school education (Zhao, Meng, 2008, p. 36; Deng, 2009, p. 11).

With the promulgation of the Law on Compulsory Education in 1986 and the implementation of the Law on the Protection of the Disabled and the Regulations of Education for People with Disabilities in 1990, an increase in the enrolment of disabled children in compulsory education became the primary task of special education. In order to save money and increase the enrolment of children with disabilities at the same time, special education classes were set up in ordinary schools in many areas in the 1980s. Meanwhile, the special educational ideas of "integration" and "mainstreaming" caused that children with disabilities were accepted for education in general classes in Beijing and Shanghai, which developed to be China's local form of implementation of inclusive education. From 1990, in order to enable children with intellectual disabilities to receive compulsory education, the placement form of learning in regular classroom appeared in rural areas as well (Mu, 2006, p. 39). In 1994, the Ministry of Education issued the Trial Approach to Carrying out Learning in the Regular Class for Children with Disabilities. Since then, Learning in Regular Classroom has gradually become the main form for disabled children of receiving compulsive education in China (Deng, 2009, p. 12).

Through decades of exploring, some new developmental patterns of special education had been initially formed by the end of the "Tenth Five-Year Plan" (2001–2005), which is characterized by a certain number of special schools as the backbone and a large number of special classes and learning in regular classes as the mainstay. According to the data of the Educational Statistics in China, there were only around 30 000 students with blindness or deafness in 292 special schools in 1978 and no schools for children with intellectual disability, nor learning in general school. But in 2001, there were about 386 400 students with special needs in schools and more than 2/3 of them were placed in general schools. There were 1 531 special schools in the whole country, among which 375 schools were for children with intellectual disabilities (Zhao, Meng, 2008, p. 37). Till the end of 2016, there were around 491 700 students with special needs in schools and more than 55 % studied in special classes in general schools or were educated in regular classes. There were 2 080 special schools in the whole country (Education Department of P.R.C., 2017).

After this half-century-long development, China has already completely established a modern school education system for special education. As shown in Figure 6, this system includes all levels of public special education and the interactive relations between different levels or forms of special education. In general, studying in special school and learning in regular

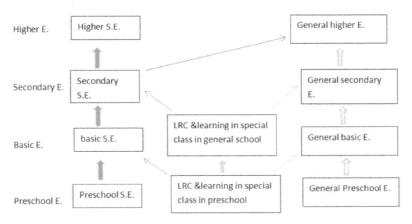

S.E. – special education; E. – education

Figure 6. The paralleled system of special education and general education in China (source: modified from a cross fusion chart of special education and general education in China, Piao, 1995, p. 57). S.E. – special education; E. – education.

classrooms or special classes in general school are two parallel approaches for children with special needs in China to receive public school education. It is also possible for students to make changes and get to the other parts.

4.1.2. Concepts of inclusive education in China

As a specialized term, inclusive education was first put forward in the Salamanca Statement at the World Conference on Special Education held by UNSCO in 1994. This new concept was based on the movement of "integration" and "mainstreaming" in western countries in the 1960s and 1970s, but it went further in emphasizing every child's uniqueness and their rights for education in regular circumstances. After this conference, the fundamental idea of inclusive education was recognized immediately by many countries and different practices of inclusive education has been tried all around the world.

Nowadays, inclusive education has been recognized as the desirable goal of the development of special education in the future and it has been written into the law or education policy in many countries. On the one hand, the wide spread of inclusive education has led to dramatic changes in the form of special education all over the world (Deng, Xiao, 2009), while on the other hand – innumerable definitions and interpretations of inclusive education exist among educators, policy makers and communities. Taking into account the different cultural backgrounds and social and economic conditions, as a approach to achieve Education for All, inclusive education may have a variety of forms and a broad range which varies from physical placement of students with special educational needs in mainstream classrooms to thorough transformations of educational system, including curricula and evaluation methods, in consideration of every child's unique characteristics, interests, abilities and learning needs (Alur, Timmons, 2009). Nowadays, inclusive education is given even a broader meaning to include many groups excluded from or marginalized within education (UNESCO, 2009). In special education, as a consensus – inclusive education is basically focused on the access and equal participation in normal educational circumstances.

Understanding of inclusive education in China

Under the influence of "integration" and "mainstreaming," inclusive education was first introduced to mainland China in the 1990s. Since then, the first confusion about inclusive education has been the translation of this new term. Inclusive education was translated into Chinese as "Rónghé jiàoyù" in Taiwan and Hongkong. In mainland China, at first inclusive education was translated as "Quán nà jiàoyù" but nowadays in order to facilitate international academic exchange, "Rónghé jiàoyù" is more and more popular and is used by researchers into special education in mainland China.

As inclusive education is a concept coming from western countries, the understanding of inclusive education by Chinese researchers is more or less based on western researchers' ideas. A Chinese inclusive education expert Huang Zhicheng points out that inclusive education is a new educational concept and also a continuous educational process, which accepts all learners (opposite to discrimination or exclusion), promotes active participation, focuses on collective cooperation and meets different needs to build an inclusive society (Huang, 2003). However, there are still different understandings of inclusive education among Chinese researchers.

Table 21. Two-dimensional analysis of inclusion (source: Lei, 2011, Introduction to Inclusive Education, Beijing University Press 2)

	One-way	Two-way
Passive	(1) one part passively waits for and accepts the other part	(3) depends on external intervention, both parts passively accept each other
Active	(2) one part actively waits for and accepts the other part	(4) both parts actively take action and accept each other

According to Li Yisheng and Cai Jun, inclusive education is a kind of education which combines the advantages of special education and general education (Li, Cai, 2003). Some Chinese researchers think that the definition of inclusive education is still not clear and it is difficult to supervise the practice in the real educational context. Inclusive education is more of a beautiful desire or philosophy of education than a clear academic concept (Liu, 2007, p. 4).

Understanding of inclusion

An important reason behind various understandings of inclusive education is the variety of different understandings of "inclusion." Therefore, one Chinese researcher tries to explain inclusive education through deep understanding of "inclusion" based on the Chinese background. He points out that, in its literal sense, "inclusion" means "integration of different parts" (Lei, 2011, p. 2). Then, the level of inclusion can be divided into four situations theoretically compliant with different traits (one-way and two-way) and intentions (active and passive) of the interaction: one-way passive inclusion, one-way active inclusion, two-way passive inclusion and two-way active inclusion (Lei, 2011, p. 2) – see Table 21.

As regards subjects of inclusive education, children with and without disabilities are the two parts of the interaction. Then one-way passive inclusion and one-way active inclusion can be divided into two sub-types: forward inclusion and reverse inclusion. Forward inclusion means that children with special needs will be integrated into normal learners group while reverse inclusion means they will wait for and accept normal students.

Both types of two-way inclusion emphasize mutual acceptance of children with and without disabilities, but the passive two-way inclusion depends on external intervention, which means some learners may be unwilling to accept each other. Then the inclusion can be superficial and it will be difficult to achieve a harmonious state even in a long run. The active two-way inclusion is based on mutual understanding and sincere acceptance of each other.

Besides the different levels of inclusion in theory, there are also different types of inclusion in practice, including partial inclusion and full inclusion in terms of the time for inclusion and sub-groups of children with special needs. Partial inclusion means that not all children with special needs are integrated into the group of general (mainstream) students or that children with disabilities are not placed into the regular classroom all the time. It depends on the practical situation with which disabilities children will be placed into the general education context with mainstream students. Meanwhile, as regards time for inclusion, partial inclusion also means placing children with disabilities into general classrooms only for some study programmes while full inclusion means that children with disabilities will be educated in general classrooms as a full-time placement (Deng, Zhu, 2007, p. 125).

Generally speaking, Chinese researchers hold a rich understanding of inclusion and try to take into consideration possibilities in both theoretical and practical levels, which helps to make the abstract concept of education real. These understandings of inclusion generate "inclusive" ideas of inclusive education comprising various forms of inclusive education practice in different cultural backgrounds and stages of social development.

Understanding of inclusive education

Inclusive education was put forward as a counterpart of segregated education. Its main purpose is eliminating segregation of children with special needs and it advocates to integrate them into the context of general education. It emphasizes all children's participation and studying with open mind and approach. On the basis of this, Chinese researchers think that there are two kinds of understanding inclusive education according to different educational subjects. The broad understanding of inclusive education focus on all children and it is now the basic concept of inclusive education in the western world, while its narrow understanding is focused on children with disabilities. The practice of inclusive education in China is based on the narrow understanding of inclusive education or, in other words, pragmatic inclusive education (Liu, 2007, p. 4).

Inclusive education is now more often discussed in the educational area, especially among special education professionals. The formation of this concept is based on much wider range of horizons, including social equity, pursuit for values, educational concept, human self-awareness, etc.

The basic idea of inclusive education is admitting the right to education as a basic human right and the foundation for social justice. Moreover, the right to education should be equal to everyone, which means not only the equal access to school, but also the same chance for educational resources and equal possibilities to meet everyone's developmental needs. Thus, the equality of education is given more meaning now than ever before, which covers equality of education at the start point, during the process and also in the outcomes. The final goal of inclusive education is to build an equal and democratic society.

From the aspect of equality at the start point, special education in segregated special schools is not really equal. Even though it ensures the right to education to children with special needs, it is still impossible for them to receive education in general schools as other students without disabilities. As regards equality during the educational process, placing children with special needs into general classroom does not naturally mean equality if suitable educational resources and methods are not provided to them. In regard to educational outcomes, equality means equal chance for success based on each student's potential, however – not the only evaluation criterion for all students. Yet, in inclusive education, equality for children with disabilities does not mean the same as for normal students at the start point, during the process or in the outcomes. There is a more important and suitable keyword in the equality for children with disabilities in inclusive education: having access to the general educational context at the start point, being taught in accordance with their aptitude and doing best of their potential.

Another outstanding feature of inclusive education is its innovative idea of human self-awareness. In traditional special education, children with special needs are entitled to compare with general students. The differences between these two groups do not only concern their level, but also the significant fact that the education for children with disabilities should be carried out in segregated special education institutions. In inclusive education, differences among people are a normal phenomenon which contributes to the uniqueness of individuals and the diversity of human beings. Unique characteristics, interests, abilities and needs should be accepted and recognized as the basis for inclusive education. The otherness of children with disabilities also should not be treated as deficits and a burden for them. Their difficulties in learning are supposed to result from interaction between children and the environment. So the way to change the situation is not only about improving children's abilities, but also about adjustment of the environment to satisfy the special educational needs of these learners (Lei, 2011, pp. 5–10).

Relations between inclusive education, special education and general education

Since inclusive education was introduced, the relation between inclusive education and special education has been an important topic among researchers. Different from the radical idea in some western countries that inclusive education should replace traditional segregated education for children with disabilities in special schools, Chinese researchers commonly hold the viewpoint that there is no conflict in essence between inclusive education and special education. They claim it is also not practical to close all special schools and place all children with disabilities in general classrooms. On the other hand, inclusive education is regarded as the bridge between special education and general education and integrate the two parts by taking advantage of each other's resources to provide high quality education for all children (Figure 7).

Moreover, special education and general education are not completely opposite to each other. Both of them have the common characteristics of the educational act and aim at cultivating people. The difference between them results from different educational objects – students with or without disabilities. Then, inclusive education seems to be the connection between these two traditionally separated educational system. It can extend to special education from the direction of arrow A or in the other direction of arrow B to general education (Lei, 2011, p. 7). Thus, inclusive education is not a single educational form, but a continuous educational system with

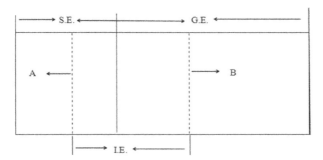

S.E. – special education, G.E. – general education, I.E. – inclusive education

Figure 7. Relations between special education, general education and inclusive education (source: Lei, 2011. Introduction to Inclusive Education. Beijing University Press 7)

S.E. – special education, G.E. – general education, I.E. – inclusive education

diverse forms at different levels of inclusion. Because of its comprehensiveness, inclusive education combines both advantages of special education and general education to meet the general and special educational needs of all children.

Based on the above understanding of inclusive education and the relations between it and special education and general education, China has developed its new practical form of providing education for children with disabilities, which is called "Suí bān jiùdú" (Learning in Regular Classroom – LRC). LRC means an educational form in which children with disabilities study in regular classroom with general students. Whether children with disabilities study in general classrooms or not is the first sign of LRC. On the other hand, if suitable education cannot be provided, even disabled children are placed in general classrooms. It cannot be counted as LRC. It means the education for learners with disabilities in general classroom should meet their special educational needs. Till now, LRC has already been widely acknowledged as the Chinese way of implementation inclusive education.

4.1.3. Learning in Regular Class (LRC) – the Chinese form of inclusive education

An interesting academic discussion about inclusive education among Chinese scholars has been around the question whether inclusive education exists in mainland China (Malinen, 2013, p. 12). The birth of LRC took place in the Chinese social context in the 1980s and was based on the influence of "integration" and "mainstreaming" in special education from the western countries. Therefore, LRC has a similar form to western "integration" and "mainstreaming," but with Chinese characteristics at the starting point, the guiding ideology, and implementation methods, etc. (Piao, 1998). For example, LRC, strongly connected to the educational thinking of Confucian philosophy and concepts of socialism, was mainly focused on children with visual impairment, hearing impairment, and intellectual disabilities at the mild level at first (Deng, Zhu, 2007; Deng, Su, 2012). Frankly speaking, LRC is the combination of the form of Western inclusive education and the reality of China's special education. It is a pragmatic and integrated educational model (Deng, Su, 2012). Looking back at the historical line of the development of special education in China, it can be found that the history of school education for children with disabilities is not long. In 1949, there were only 2 380 students with deafness or blindness in 42 special schools in the whole country. Most of the special schools were founded by foreign missionaries or charity institutions, which means special schools were more likely to be located in cities of the East or central parts of China with better economic situation and more open social atmosphere.

After the foundation of PRC, some measures were taken to develop special education by the government. The overall image of special schools and the shortage of schools for children with disabilities had been an actual problem for a long time. Many disabled children could not receive school education as special schools were too far away, which was even worse in western part or rural areas of China with their limited financial resources, lack of expertise and bad transportation conditions. Yet, at the same time, the desire for education of children with special needs constituted an actual demand. Hence, general schools seemed to be the only choice for children with disabilities to receive some education. In the 1950s, some general schools started to accept disabled children to the regular classrooms as a fragmentary attempt in some rural areas of western China (Sheng, 2011, p. 192).

The systematic practice of admitting children with disabilities into regular classrooms of general schools started in the 1980s, along with the advancement of Chinese legislation which emphasized ensuring equal rights for people with disabilities and also started to support a more inclusive approach in education (Deng, Manset, 2000; Deng, Poon-Mcbrayer, Farnsworth, 2001). In 1987, in order to solve the problem of enrolment in compulsory education for children with disabilities, the Chinese government conducted a pilot study of placing children with disabilities into mainstream classrooms in 15 counties. The pilot study started for children with hearing impairment and visual impairment at first and then covered children with mild intellectual disability (Xiao, 2005, pp. 3–4). Accepting children with disabilities in mainstream classes was then determined as the national policy for developing special education at the first national special education conference in 1988. Two years later, the new government policy was given the name "suíbān jiùdú" (Learning in Regular Classrooms – LRC).

Later, the Chinese government carried out more pilot studies to explore the implementation of LRC. In 1994, the Ministry of Education issued the official regulation named Trial Measures on Carrying out Learning in Regular Classroom for Disabled Children which symbolized the final formation of Chinese way of inclusive education: LRC. As it has been already stated, since then, LRC has gradually become the main placement for children with special needs to receive compulsory education in China.

As a local mode of implementing inclusive education, LRC appeared in the China's unique state condition in a specific historical stage and developed alongside the advancement of local society. Meanwhile, the specific measures of implementing LRC have also been adjusted to keep in line with the requirements of inclusive education.

4.1.4. Cultural determinants of LRC

As a part of social life, any kind of educational concept or act cannot be isolated from certain cultural background and social state. Inclusive education as a new educational concept borrowed from the Western world is also based on the cultural and social background of western countries, which symbolizes the Western social foundations of diversity and equal opportunity and the philosophical tradition of liberation. It aims at ensuring that children with special needs have equal access to free and appropriate education in general school with fully abled children as well as at building an inclusive and equal society. Correspondingly, LRC in China is also based on the Chinese cultural background and social and economic situation.

Moral ideas of Confucianism

Created by Confucius more than 2000 years ago, Confucianism has become the mainstream of traditional Chinese culture and it has brought far-reaching effects on China and East Asia. On the one hand, Confucianism emphasizes the function of education and puts education at the first place in building the country and social management. On the other hand, systematic school education for people with disabilities has never come into being in the long history of the Chinese feudal society, dominated by the Confucian thought.

By analysing the social views of Confucianism, it can be stated that quality for everyone has never been the value pursued by it. As regards the social management in the idea of Confucianism, people belong to four different classes: "Shì" (intellectual class), "nóng" (peasant class), "gōng"(working class), "shāng" (business class). Among the four classes, "Shì" is the highest level, comprising those who are supposed to govern the country, while "shāng" is the lowest level. The aim of education for Confucianism is to cultivate the elite named "Jūnzǐ," who have excellent morality and are good at management of their home and the country. The key requirement of "Jūnzǐ" is "Rén," which means benevolence and is shown by kindness to another person. People with disabilities belong to the ground class of the society and are the target for higher classes of showing their empathy and morality (Hou, 2001). However, on the other hand, Confucianism also puts forward rich educational suggestions, which include ensuring individuals from any class the access to education and teaching students according to their personal characteristics.

In general, the inconsistent moral ideas of Confucianism constitute the cultural background of Chinese inclusive education. On one hand, the moral ideas of Confucianism had resulted in the unwanted situation that disabled people were excluded from the educational system in the past. On the other hand, it has the deeply rooted idea of caring for people with disabilities in Chinese people's minds. In the past, people with disabilities are supposed to be a disadvantaged group and abnormal minority of the society, who are vulnerable to be discriminated by the majority.

Then, the idea of caring for disabled people was reflected by various preferential treatments, including reduced taxes, providing reliefs, arranging care institutions, and so on. Nowadays, this idea is to a large extent reflected by the action of sharing social civilization with this minority group and ensuring equal educational rights and resources to children with special needs according to the policies of the Chinese government. Moreover, it should be noticed that moral ideas with the function of guiding people's behaviour cannot be the guaranteed for exceptional children's equal educational rights. There is still a long way to improve the law system for inclusive education in China.

Value orientations of pragmatism

As the Chinese way of practicing inclusive education, LRC was first put forward in the 1980s. It was affected by the development of special education in western countries, but its original purpose was to solve the problem that many children with special needs had no access to school education. In the 1980s, along with the economic development and social advancement resulting from the policy of Reform and Opening, the legal system for education gradually developed in China. In 1986, the Compulsory Education Law of People's Republic of China was issued by the Chinese government. According to this law, compulsory education is for all school-age children and it is a public welfare measure undertaken and guaranteed by the state. Obviously, school-age children with special educational needs are also included into the group of children for compulsory education. On the basis of this law, receiving education is not only a right but also an obligation to all children at school age, including children with disabilities.

Nevertheless, according to the statistics from the Ministry of Education, there were only 504 special schools with 52 000 students in 1987. It was estimated that there were about 6.5 million children with disabilities at the age 1 to 15 years, which was based on the data from the first survey of people with disabilities in the same year. This means that around 6.45 million school-age children with special needs were excluded from educational institutions at that time. Therefore, improving the enrolment ratio of disabled children became an urgent task. Considering the limited financial situation, it was not possible to build enough special schools for all children with special needs. Affected also by the movement of "mainstreaming" and "integration" in special education in western countries, the placement of disabled children in the nearest general schools came as the most effective way for struggling against the shortage of special educational institutions and for increasing the enrolment quickly. Hence, it was pointed out that LRC is a pragmatic and also inevitable choice to improve special education in China as a developing country with underdeveloped conditions of economy and culture (Deng, Poon-McBrayer, 2013). It can be said that LRC is the practical form of special education which was explored by Chinese special education professionals in compliance with China's national conditions. LRC has enriched the implementation forms of special education in China and has become the major service delivery model to universal compulsory education for Chinese children with disabilities (Deng, Poon-McBrayer, 2013).

Based on the value orientations of pragmatism, LRC did not cover all children with special needs. When it was introduced, only three categories (children with hearing impairment, visual impairment and mild intellectual disability) had the access to learning in regular classroom on the assumption that these three kinds are easier to adapt to the studying in the general education context. As the original purpose of LRC was to raise the enrolment of children with disabilities, putting children into general classroom was the prior or the only standard for LRC. The importance of "in regular classroom" was far more highly estimated than "learning" for a long time. This mistaken understanding resulted in a worsening situation of actual learning for some students with disabilities in China, which was called "Sitting in Regular Classroom" or "passing time in regular classroom." However, also because the value orientation behind LRC is pragmatic, the implementation of this educational form has been flexible according to the needs in the practice. Along with the development of special education in China in the past decades, more categories of children with special needs have been placed to study in general classrooms. On the other hand, improving the quality of LRC has already become a more urgent task in the implementation of inclusive education in China.

4.2. Inclusive education in practice

In the last decades, China has always taken LRC as a very important form of providing educational service to children with disabilities. The implementation of LRC has been proved to be a useful and effective measure in practice in the Chinese environment. However, there are still some unsolved barriers to be explored and eliminated in the future.

4.2.1. Development of LRC

In contrast to the development of special education in some Western counties, the inclusive education proponents in China have never attempted to eliminate special schools and classes. Even though special schools represent the typical segregated special education placement and LRC is widely regarded as the Chinese model of implementing inclusive education, China has successfully formed a three-tier service delivery system, which consists of an array of placement options of special schools, special classes and LRC to serve students with disabilities (Deng, Zhu, 2016, p. 995). This three-tier service delivery system is often described as "Yǐ tèshū jiàoyù xuéxiào wèi gǔgàn, yǐ suíbān jiùdú hé tèjiào bān wéi zhǔtǐ" (Special education school as backbone, learning in regular classroom or special classrooms in general school as the main body) and has been legally consolidated in all laws and government regulations regarding special education since 1990s. In this system, the roles of both special education schools and LRC are emphasized and these types of education are regarded as responsible for providing educational service for a huge number of children with special needs.

Based on the Compulsory Education Law of PRC passed in 1986 and the Trial Measures of Implementing Learning in Regular Classrooms for Children and Adolescents with Disabilities in 1994, LRC dramatically developed in the 1990s in China and students with disabilities have been increasingly educated in regular classrooms. In 1992, there were only 129 400 disabled students educated in schools and 28 % (36 558 students) of them were in general classrooms in 1992 (Deng, Zhu, 2016, p. 995). However, in 2016, there were 491 740 students with disabilities in schools, among whom more than one half (55.06 %) studied in general schools. Moreover, 1,521 new students were recruited, among whom 56.6 % were placed in mainstreaming educational institutions including mainstream classrooms or special classes in general schools (Ministry of Education of PRC, 2017).

According to the data presented below (Table 22), the percentage of students enrolled for special education services in general schools have

Table 22. Overall development of special education in China from 1994–2016 (source: data of 1994–2012 is from the China Institute of Educational Finance Research, 2013, http://ciefr.pku.edu.cn/cbw/kyjb/2016/kyjb_8180.shtml; data of 2013–2016 is from the Ministry of Education of People's Republic of China; data of 2013–2016 is from the Ministry of Education of People's Republic of China, National Education Development Bulletin).

Year	No. of special schools	No. of enrolled students for special education services (unit: 10,000)			Percentage of students in general schools
		In total	No. of students in general schools	No. of students in special schools	
1994	1241	21.14	11.53	9.61	54.54
1995	1379	29.56	17.73	11.83	59.98
1996	1426	32.11	19.51	12.6	60.76
1997	1440	34.06	21.15	12.91	62.10
1998	1535	35.84	22.55	13.29	62.92
1999	1520	37.16	23.64	13.52	63.62
2000	1539	37.76	23.93	13.83	63.37
2001	1531	38.64	26.99	11.65	69.86
2002	1540	37.45	25.57	11.88	68.29
2003	1551	36.47	24.15	12.32	66.23
2004	1560	37.18	24.30	12.88	65.35
2005	1593	36.44	23.00	13.44	63.13
2006	1605	36.29	22.18	14.11	61.12
2007	1618	41.93	27.20	14.73	64.88
2008	1640	41.74	26.14	15.33	63.27
2009	1672	42.81	26.91	15.9	62.87
2010	1706	42.56	25.96	16.6	60.99
2011	1767	39.87	22.52	17.35	56.48
2012	1853	37.88	19.98	17.90	52.74
2013	1933	36.81	19.08	17.73	51.84
2014	2000	39.49	20.91	18.58	52.94
2015	2053	44.22	23.96	20.26	54.20
2016	2080	49.17	27.08	22.09	55.06

always been higher than 50 % with the highest number of 69.86 % in the last 24 years. It can be said that as the local model of practicing inclusive education in China, LRC has become the main approach for providing educational services in response to the international trend of inclusive education and the domestic need of serving possibly the largest numbers of children with disabilities (Deng, Harris, 2008).

By doing further analysis of the data concerning LRC students in 2016, the distribution of children with special needs who study in general classrooms varies in regard to different disability types and learning phases.

As shown in Table 23, in terms of disability, LRC students comprise four types, among which children with intellectual disabilities are the majority of LRC students with the percentage of 42.9 %. Other disabilities including learning disabilities and emotional and behaviour disabilities also share more than 1/3 of all LRC students. However, as the disabilities were first taken into consideration in placing in mainstreaming schools, the number of children with hearing impairment and visual impairment in regular schools is relatively smaller.

Besides this, in the whole 9 years of compulsive education, there are 2.5 times more LRC students in primary school than secondary school. Considering different grades of these two phases, the average number of LRC students in each grade of primary school is 32,099 and the average number in secondary school is 24,951, which means around 22.2 % of LRC students dropped out after primary general school. Some researchers point out that it is harder for LRC students to adapt to the learning

Table 23. Basic statistics of LRC students in 2016 (unit: person) (source: adapted from Ministry of education of the People's Republic of China (2017) – Education Statistics of 2016; http://www.moe.gov.cn/s78/A03/moe_560/jytjsj_2016/2016_qg/201708/t20170823_311710.html)

	HI	VI	ID	Other	In total
Primary school	20846	17874	88682	65196	192598
Junior secondary school	7579	9545	26176	31554	74854
In total	28425	27419	114858	96750	267452

requirements in a higher study phase. As a result, they have to drop out from general schools and flow back to special schools.

Another important feature in the development of inclusive education in China is the relation between LRC and special schools. China has promoted inclusive education which does not aim at deconstructing the existing special education school system, but acts simultaneously with its development. On the one hand, the number of special schools has been almost continuously increasing from 504 to 2080 from 1985 to 2016 (Ministry of Education of PRC). On the other hand, the development of LRC in China has stimulated transformations in the function of special schools. Special education schools are more expected to be educational institutions to provide special education service for children with profound disabilities and resource centres to support general schools which serve the majority of children with special educational needs (Zhu, Wang, 2011).

4.2.2. Organization of LRC

The practice of inclusive education in mainland China (LRC) and its running depends on the top-down administration, which means that the related laws and regulations are critical to the implementation of LRC. The right of children with special needs to study in mainstream school was first admitted by The People's Republic of China Compulsory Education Law in 1986. It said that "General school should accept disabled children who have the ability to receive general education in regular classrooms and should provide support for their study and rehabilitation" (Ministry of Educatiion, 1986). In 1994, this right was confirmed again in the Disability Education Regulations of PRC, which said that "age-appropriate children can receive compulsory education in mainstream classrooms according to the conditions" (State Council of PRC,1994). In the same year, the most important official regulation about LRC in mainland China – the Trial Measures on Carrying out Learning in Regular Classrooms for Children with Disabilities – was issued by the Ministry of Education. Many concrete terms of how to carry out inclusive education were put forward in this regulation, including objects, admission, management, and so on (Ministry of Education, 1994).

4.2.3. Eligibility for LRC

As the original aim of LRC is to increase the enrolment into compulsive education of children with disabilities, the objects of LRC are children with disabilities, especially children with hearing impairment (including deafness and hearing impairment), visual impairment (including blindness and low vision) and children with mild intellectual disabilities. Children with moderate intellectual disabilities can also be included in school education under certain conditions. Thus, hearing impairment, visual impairment and intellectual disabilities are officially accepted objects of LRC. Moreover, also because of this restriction of LRC's objects, LRC has been criticized as contrary to the basic concept of inclusive education for all children.

Along with the development of LRC in practice, the objects of LRC have been broadened to other disabilities including autism spectrum disorder, ADHD, other emotional and behavioural disorders, etc., which consisted a large part of all LRC students in 2016 according to data in the above presented Table XX. In addition, some cities including Beijing, Shanghai, Guangzhou, Dujiangyan, formulated local regulations to promote the development of LRC based on the national policy, in which the objects of LRC included the whole 7 types of disabilities according to the central government standards of disability.

Apart from this, large numbers of children with learning disabilities, speech and language disorders, physical disabilities had studied in regular classrooms in China for a long time before the policy of LRC was introduced (Xing, 2015, p. 9). Moreover, influenced by the development of inclusive education in the Western world, the Chinese practice of LRC has also absorbed the core concepts of inclusive education which emphasize the equal right of education for children with special needs and the unique characteristics of every individual. In a nutshell, we can say that LRC was originally put forward to provide compulsive education for children with disabilities in China in the 1980s but later has evolved to be the Chinese approach in the implementation of inclusive education.

4.2.4. Admission to LRC

According to the national policy, children with disabilities should be placed in the nearest general schools in the school district. Still, in the city or area with convenient transportation, a relatively concentrated placement in certain schools can be accepted as well. General schools must admit disabled children who have the abilities to study in regular classrooms within the school district. The admission age for LRC students is the same as for ordinary students and can be properly postponed only in exceptional conditions. The number of LRC students in one regular classroom is supposed to be controlled – 1 or 2 and no more than 3 students with disabilities (Xing, 2015, p. 246).

Moreover, there are special rules for labelling LRC students and LRC students' personal information is forbidden to be disclosed for protection of privacy. For example, in Guangzhou children with special needs will be labelled as LRC students at the 2nd grade, except the children with obvious disabilities including hearing impairment, visual impairment or physical impairment. In Shanghai the labelling time is the 3rd grade. The reason for this rule is to give more time for teachers, parents and other professionals to observe the adaptation of disabled children in general schools and to reduce the wrong judgment of eligibility for LRC. Moreover, the eligibility for children with disabilities attending regular classrooms will be reviewed every two years and those children who do not meet the disability standards any more will be de-labelled of LRC students.

4.2.5. Management of LRC

In China, the local government is responsible for the management and implementation of LRC based on the general regulations from the central government. As a result, the local governments in different provinces and municipalities have developed different regulations depending on the local situation. Yet, there is some consensus of various local management regulations concerning LRC. The first issue is that the implementation of LRC should be included into the management system of special education and general education. Despite the placement of LRC students in general school, the service for LRC students requires cooperation of general school, special school and special education resource centre. The responsibilities of the three parts should be clearly distinguished in the development of LRC. Taking the local regulations from one municipality as an example, the responsibilities of the three parts are as follows:

The responsibilities of general school in the practice of LRC

1. Establishing a working group composed of principals, teaching directors, grade leaders, head teachers and teachers of different subjects. The working group is responsible for developing specific management rules in general school.
2. Designing courses, arranging learning content, learning time and teaching methods for LRC students according to their actual needs and ensuring an individual education and rehabilitation training time for each student.
3. Making sure of the objects of LRC and arranging the suitable placement in compliance with the actual situation of the LRC students.
4. Formulating multiple evaluation content which is suitable for the characteristics of LRC students and reflects the process of the learners' development and conducting comprehensive evaluation of the development of LRC students.
5. Organizing a research group to carry out school-based research on teaching LRC students.
6. Ensuring the facilities needed for special education, establishing an equal, caring and friendly relationship between students and teachers, integrating special education into the school culture, making full use of and developing various educational resources that help students with disabilities to learn, and creating a good environment that is accessible and can enhance students' development.
7. Carrying out the teaching training for teachers who work with LRC students and forming a group of teachers who are good at working in regular classrooms with children with disabilities.
8. Establishing a contact system between parents and school, carrying out a variety of guidance activities concerning family education, and promptly taking into consideration parents' opinions and suggestions for the practice of LRC.
9. Under the guidance of a special education centre in the district, giving timely feedback on LRC students and some reports on the practice of LRC.

The responsibilities of special education resource centre in the practice of LRC

1. Being responsible for the auditing of the eligibility of LRC students in the area as well as the administration of student registration, and establishing a personal file for each LRC student for follow-up management.

2. Supervising the work of LRC in general school including giving suggestions on the placement of LRC students, curriculum arrangement, education and teaching management, evaluation content and methods, and allocation of educational resources; conducting technical guidance on the formulation and implementation of individual educational plan (IEP), rehabilitation training, education and teaching, and providing regular or irregular rehabilitation for LRC students with special rehabilitation needs.

3 Carrying out prospective research into LRC, studying the hot spots and difficulties in the management of LRC, education and teaching, rehabilitation training, etc., at the same time summarizing and promoting teachers' advanced experience and research results concerning LRC work.

4. Undertaking the training of teachers who carry out LRC practice to improve their related abilities and promote their professional development; conducting the training for parents of LRC students and promoting cooperation between parents and school to contribute to the development of LRC students.

5. Carrying out the database construction including collecting, organizing and producing rich texts, images and audio-visual materials for teachers and parents to provide a relevant special education policy, theoretical special education knowledge, the latest achievements in special education research and useful experience from schools' practice of LRC to build a platform for the exchange of information.

6. Making use of the advantages of professionals, facilities and equipment of the special education centre to provide various services due to the actual needs of schools, teachers, parents and students; helping teachers and parents to solve practical problems in the process of education and teaching.

The responsibilities of special education school in the practice of LRC

1. Taking advantage of the resources including special education teachers and rehabilitation facilities in special school to provide technical support and services for the practice of LRC; assisting the Special Education Center in carrying out rehabilitation training for LRC students and skills training and guidance for teachers in general school and LRC students' parents.
2. Maximizing the expertise of teaching and research in special school by conveying their successful experience in teaching and rehabilitation to general school and playing the role of the backbone in guiding general school to improve the quality of teaching for LRC students.
3. Taking part in the work of auditing the eligibility of LRC students, assisting the Special Education Center in guiding the rehabilitation training and individualized education for LRC students in general school, and helping teachers in general school to improve knowledge and skills of special education.

Generally speaking, as regards the implementation of LRC, general school is the environment for the placement of LRC students and carrying out direct teaching and rehabilitation training. Teachers in general school are the direct providers of education for disabled children in regular classrooms under the professional guidance of special education resource centre supported by professional personnel and facilities from special school. In practice, special education centres are often set up in special schools and outstanding special education teachers with rich experience serve as staff there.

4.2.6. Combined regular and special curriculum for LRC learners

According to the regulations on LRC issued by the Chinese central government, children with disabilities who are eligible for learning in regular classrooms are children who can adapt to the study in mainstream schools with additional special education support. Hence, LRC students in the mainstream classrooms are supposed to implement the regular curriculum and to use the same textbooks as other students with disabilities. Yet, the learning requirements should be adjusted to the actual needs of LRC students. However, children with disabilities may also need some special courses according to their different disabilities and educational needs.

(1) *Two options for LRC learners to study the regular curriculum*

Depending on the condition of LRC students and the requirements of the ordinary curriculum, adaptation to the regular curriculum and adjustment to it are the two options for LRC students to study in regular classrooms.

Adaptation to ordinary curriculum requires from LRC students studying the same contents and attaining corresponding teaching goals based on some additional support and services. In this way, children with disabilities are supposed to master all the knowledge and skills as ordinary students. The teacher will not adjust the content of curriculum and the goals of teaching for LRC students but will change the way of providing the teaching materials and assessing these students' learning performance according to the students' learning characteristics (Li, 2013, pp. 193–195).

In particular, there are many measures to support LRC students' based on practical experience, including giving more time and exercise opportunities to LRC students, providing appropriate learning materials and equipment, presenting teaching materials in multiple ways, and so on. For example, students with low vision may be provided with visual aids and textbooks with bigger characters or relatively quiet seats may be arranged for children with emotional problems.

Adjustment to the regular curriculum means that LRC students will study the regular curriculum, but the content of curriculum and the goals of learning will be adjusted to students' actual needs and the characteristics of the ordinary curriculum. The adjustment of ordinary curriculum includes modifications of teaching contents and expected students' performance. On the one hand, teachers can adjust the amount and scope of the teaching content to ensure that LRC students can master the critical content of the curriculum. On the other hand, teachers can also decrease the difficulty level and depth of the teaching content to adjust the expected performance of LRC students.

(2) *Special curriculum for students with different disabilities*

Students with disabilities in mainstream classrooms, apart from the regular curriculum, may also need a special curriculum on the condition that the regular curriculum cannot meet their educational needs. The special curriculum should be arranged on the basis of LRC students' actual needs, which vary among students with different types of disability. For example, children with visual impairment may need an extra special course in the braille and mobility orientation, while children with hearing impairment in regular classrooms may need an extra oral and language training course and children with intellectual disabilities may need an extra course in social adaptation and self-care skills.

(3) *Principles of arranging curriculum for LRC students*

No matter which approach to the curriculum implementation is undertaken, there are some basic principles of arranging the curriculum for LRC students on the basis of adequate evaluation of their educational needs (Li, 2013, p. 197):

A. Comprehensive development should be emphasized in the process of arranging the curriculum and the teaching contents should include at least three areas in regard to knowledge, skills and emotions.
B. A functional curriculum should be taken into consideration and the content of curriculum should be related to students' real life.
C. Thematic courses should be developed to stimulate students' motivation to learn.
D. Students' perception level should be considered during the process of arranging the curriculum.
E. The curriculum contents should be flexible enough to meet different educational needs of students.
F. The integrity and correctness of the curriculum should be ensured without destroying the logical structure of the course.
G. It is better to develop a curriculum for all students in the classroom and not to segregate and separate LRC students from their classmates.

As regards the implementation of LRC in different schools, local governments give more flexibility for arranging curricula and choosing textbook for students with disabilities. General schools can also choose textbooks from special schools or use general school teaching materials for LRC students. In general, the teaching requirements for children with hearing or visual impairment are the same as those for regular students, and moderate adjustment is also possible under special conditions. The teaching contents for students with intellectual disabilities may be appropriately arranged in reference to teaching plans, syllabuses and teaching materials in special education school. Some local policies ask teachers to determine the difficulty level and decide what amount of content can be dynamically taken from the curriculum for ordinary students in compliance with actual learning abilities of LRC students. General school should also develop school-based teaching materials for rehabilitation or instruction of life skills to LRC students except those who implement the general education curriculum.

A study on the implementation of LRC in Shanghai conducted in 2011 shows that, among 300 general schools with disabled students, only 3 schools set a small part of the extra curriculum for LRC students, while children with disabilities in 281 general schools studied the same curriculum as fully-abled students all the time in regular classrooms. LRC students in 18 schools studied almost the same courses in regular classrooms and a small part of the same curriculum was implemented separately (Yu, 2011, p. 5). The researcher pointed out that most of the general schools had not set or adjusted the curriculum to the needs of children with disabilities in the practice of LRC.

4.2.7. Financial mechanisms of LRC

The level of the funding input plays a key role in the development of special education. In order to know the financial mechanism of LRC, it is needed to have a rough understanding of the financial situation of special education in China.

Financial input for special education

For a long time, the financial input, social contributions and tuition fees have been the three sources of special education funding, among which the financial input from the government is the main source that accounts for more than 97 % of the total. Social contribution takes only a slight part of less than 1 % (Tian et al., 2015, p. 36). In recent years, the country has carried out a new policy called "Two Exemptions and One Supplement" (the exemption of tuition and textbook fee and the subsidy for accommodation) to support all children with disabilities during the compulsive education period. Since then, the tuition fee has no longer been a source of funding for special education.

The financial input for special education mainly depends on the input from the local government and is supplemented by the input from the central government. Therefore, the development of special education is largely related to the level of local economic development, which in turn has brought about large regional differences in the development of special education in different areas.

The input from the central government is called the dedicated funding for special education and it has been continuously increasing for a long time (Xie et al., 2009, p. 22). According to some recent research, the dedicated financial input from the central government is 0.41 billion Yuan for each year from 2014 to 2016. It was 12 million in 2008 and 50 million in 2012. The expenditure of special schools increased more than 8 times from 0.84 billion to 7.67 billion over 14 years from 1998 to 2011. The growth rate was similar to the increase in total expenditure for education from 266.89 billion to 2,308.58 billion (Tian et al., 2015, p. 36). Yet, the percentage of expenditure for special schools is less than 0.35 % in the total expenditure for education.

On the other hand, along with the increase of total financial input from the government and the low proportion of expenditure for special school, the financial input for every student in special school as regards Average Education Funding and Average Public Funding has been much higher than for every student in general middle school with 4–6 times more of Average Education Funding and 5–7 times more of Average Public Funding (Tian et al., 2015, p. 37).

From 2014, Chinese government had implemented the Special Education Promotion Plan (2014–2016) (hereinafter referred to as the "first-phase plan"), in which the Average Public Funding for students in special school was planned to increase to at least 6000 Yuan/year for one student till 2016. Currently, the Average Public Funding is 650 Yuan/year for a primary school student and 850 Yuan/year for a general secondary school student. From 2017, along with the publishing of the second Special Education Promotion Plan (2017–2020), the Average Public Funding for special education students has further increased in some areas, for example 10 times to the funding for a general secondary school student in Qingdao city of

Shandong province and 15 times to the funding for a general student in Wenzhou city of Zhejiang province.

Financial input for LRC

According to the analysis above, the Chinese government has invested a considerable amount of funding for the development of special education. However, from the point of the used funding, vast majority of the money has been given to special schools. LRC, as the main body to provide special education services to students with disabilities, lacks a funding guarantee as a corresponding funding mechanism has not been established (Tian et al., 2015, p. 37; Xie et al., 2009, p. 22).

Issued in 1994, the Trial Measures of Implementing Learning in Regular Class-rooms for Children and Adolescents with Disabilities is the only specialized document pertaining to LRC in China and includes comprehensive contents on the implementation of LRC. In this document, educational administrative departments at all levels are asked to gradually increase the funding for disabled children educated in regular classrooms and consider the actual needs of LRC and provide convenience in terms of teacher position, workload accounting, teaching aids, coursebooks, etc. Still, there was no detailed information about financial support for the implementation of LRC in this Trial Measure from the central government. In 2010, the Chinese central government issued an important policy document called Guidelines for Mid-term and Long-term Education Reform and Development (2010–2020), which gave freedom to local governments to decide about the standard of average funding for each disabled student. Therefore, the financial input for LRC is in close relation to the local government and varies a lot among different regions.

Even though there is no national funding statistics for LRC at present, the current research shows that financial support for LRC in East territories is better than in the Western ones, which is similar to the financial funding to the overall special education in the whole country (Wang, Yang, Zhang, 2006, p. 5; Wei, Qi, Zhao, 2016, p. 126). A considerable percentage of general schools in the Western area of China has never got a dedicated fund for LRC (Tian et al., 2015, p. 37). Moreover, only a small amount of financial investment to LRC in general schools is mainly used for the construction of resource rooms.

In addition, there is no clear regulation of the subsidy for teachers who work with disabled children in general classrooms from the central government, while there has been a long history of subsidies for special education teachers in special schools since 1956. According to the regulation from the central government, special education teachers can get extra 15 % of the total of teachers' basic salary, depending on their level of position, which is called a special education allowance. On the basis of the central government standards, different provinces and areas have set different standards of the special education allowance according to their practical situation, mostly between 15 % and 30 % with the highest of 50 %. For example, the standard of the allowance for special education teachers in Beijing City and provinces of Xinjiang, Shanxi, Qinghai is 15 %, while the allowance for special education teachers in Guandong province is 30 % and 50 % in Shanxi province (Tian et al., 2015, p. 38). In some areas, the allowance for special education teachers depends on the length of teachers' work time in special schools.

In practice, a subsidy for teachers who work with disabled students in general schools also varies from place to place. In some areas, there are small subsidies for inclusive teachers while no subsidy in some other areas at all. For example, a full-time resource teacher in Beijing can get allowances for special education as teachers who work in special school, which is always 15 % of the salary according to their position, and a main teacher who works with disabled students in general classroom can get 50 Yuan/month as the extra allowance, while other teachers who just teach one subject to disabled students cannot get any allowance. Yet, there is no extra allowance for teachers who work with disabled students in Lanzhou city and Zhangye city in the northwest part of China. Generally speaking, the majority of teachers who work with disabled students in general schools are given no extra allowance (Save the Children, 2012, p. 11).

The lack of clear regulations pertaining to workload accounting and an insufficient extra allowance for teachers who work with disabled students in general schools should not be underestimated as it can decrease teachers' motivation for accepting disabled students to their classrooms and can undermine the further development of inclusive education.

Fortunately, the Chinese central government has given further explanation of the financial support for LRC in some official regulations

on education or special education in recent years. Both in the Special
Education Promotion Plan (2014–2016) and the second Special Education
Promotion Plan (2017–2020), there are specific contents concerning the
average fund for LRC students. According to these two plans, the average
funding for disabled students in special schools during the compulsory
education should be no less than 6000 Yuan/year and the average funding
for disabled students who learn in regular classrooms or special classrooms
in general schools during compulsory education is the same as for students
in special schools. Moreover, the local governments are asked to provide
more financial support to students with disabilities and free high school
education to disabled children from families in poverty. For example,
the local government in Shuangliu area of Chengdu city has given general schools extra 100 Yuan/year for each disabled student to be used as
teacher training fee since 2008. In addition, each disabled student from a
poor family in general school can get 80 Yuan/month for meals (Save the
Children, 2012, p. 11). Still, as the main approach to provide special education services to the majority of students with disabilities, LRC should be
given more financial investment to ensure high quality of education (Xie
et al., 2009, p. 23; Tian et al., 2015, p. 39).

4.2.8. Competences and qualifications of
inclusive education teachers

As they are people who directly work with students at school, the importance of teachers for students' development should not be undervalued.
In the Warnock Report from the UK, teachers are regarded as those who
play a significant role in the process of delivering both special and inclusive
education, which can become challenging and difficult due to the diverse
needs of children with disabilities, especially those with severe or multiplied conditions (Department of Education and Science of UK, 1978,
p. 107). Therefore, inclusive education teachers have been regarded as an
important component in the success of inclusive education practice and
the issues of the qualifications for inclusive education teachers have gained
a lot of concern worldwide (Forlin, Chambers, 2010; Sanrattana, 2010;
Vaillant, 2011).

In 2000, the United Nations Children's Fund pointed out the necessity of adequately educated and trained teachers in the process of

delivering high quality education for all children through the paper entitled "Defining Quality in Education" (United Nations Children's Fund,
2000, p. 14). In 2015, United Nations Educational, Scientific and Cultural
Organization issued the Incheon Declaration and clearly stated that it is
necessary for all teachers as well as educators to be well-trained and sufficiently recruited, to possess professional qualifications, have their own
empowerment and motivation, and receive support under the systems
which are well-supplied, productively governed and efficient so that they
are well-prepared and fully-equipped with sufficient knowledge and skills
to deliver good quality education and enhance the learning outcomes of all
learners. Correspondingly, the qualifications for special education teachers
and inclusive education teachers have become a hot topic for Chinese education researchers for a long time (Lei, Yao, 2005; Meng, 2008; Wang,
Hu, 2008).

In China, special education teachers are teachers who educate students
with disabilities in special schools, while inclusive education teachers
work with disabled students and mostly also with non-disabled students
as well in general schools. According to the Chinese implementation of
inclusive education (LRC), there are three kinds of inclusive education
teachers: general teachers who directly work with disabled students in general classrooms – called LRC teachers, resource room teachers who are
responsible for supporting disabled students in all schools, and itinerant
teachers from special school or outside special education resource centres
who are responsible for disabled students in several general schools (Feng,
2014, p. 4).

Qualification for LRC teachers

As students with disabilities are placed in general classrooms, LRC teachers
are the majority of inclusive education teachers and they directly work
with students. Their qualifications are vital to the academic performance
and comprehensive development of students with disabilities.

According to the Trial Measures of Implementing Learning in Regular
Classrooms for Children and Adolescents with Disabilities issued in 1994,
teachers who work with disabled students in general classrooms should be
chosen from general teachers who are willing to work with disabled children and have good teacher morality and high qualifications. They are also

required to have basic knowledge and skills in special education and know basic teaching principles and methods in inclusive education.

In practice, usually LRC teachers are in-service excellent general teachers who are willing to work with disabled students and they have already finished some courses of special education during their university studies or will be asked to take part in some training program of special education when they start to be LRC teachers (Ma, Tan, 2010, p. 62).

At present, there are still no detailed qualifications for LRC teachers for the whole country. Yet, in different areas, local governments have issued their local regulations based on the general requirement from the central government. For example, in Shanghai, LRC teachers are required to accomplish a training course in special education and also acquire teacher qualification in the subjects they teach before starting to be LRC teachers.

Qualification for resource room teachers

As an important placement of children with disabilities in the practice of inclusive education, the resource room program (RRP) has also become a vital part of the support system of LRC in China. Therefore, besides LRC teachers, resource teachers are the second type of inclusive education teachers. A resource room teacher (RRT) is the main staff in the resource room and is responsible for various tasks concerning the implementation of inclusive education, including the assessment and plan development, resource teaching, consulting, day-to-day management, etc. (Wang, 2005, p. 38). In the practice of RRP, RRTs are regarded to have the core positions as the bridge between special education and general education (Wang, Xiao, 2017, p. 33).

In 2016, the Education Department of China issued the Construction Guide of Special Education Resource Room in General School to specify the details about RRP in general school. According to this document, the resource room should be given priority in general schools to organize education for more disabled students and keep them for a long period in the local school adjustment plan. General schools that recruit more than 5 disabled students should establish resource rooms. In the case of fewer than 5 disabled students, the local educational administrations should plan the layout of resource rooms to ensure service for all the disabled students.

RRTs are required to have a theoretical background in special education, rehabilitation or other related majors, and to be in line with the academic qualifications and the corresponding teacher certificate mentioned in the "Teacher Law." They have to meet the requirements of the "Professional Standard for Special Education Teachers." In addition, pre-job training is also necessary to ensure them with basic theory, specialist knowledge, and operating skills of special education and rehabilitation training. RRTs in Shanghai are required to have the Shanghai Special Education Position Certificate, which means RRTs should have both the general teacher certificate and special education certificate.

Qualification for itinerant teachers

As an important element in the guarantee system for supporting inclusive education, itinerant teaching has gradually become a common practice to promote the development of inclusive education in the world. In the process of implementation of itinerant teaching, itinerant teachers play the key roles, as they are significant supporters of disabled children's learning in regular classes and they determine the educational effect of these children's learning (Zhang, Wang, 2017, p. 3).

In practice, itinerant teachers are the professional staff engaged in directing special education work and conducting periodic or special tutoring for children with disabilities in a number of schools, families, and hospitals in a region by roving teaching. In China, itinerant teachers are mostly teachers from special schools or special education resource centres who are often attached to special schools. The qualifications of itinerant teachers mainly depend on the teachers' qualifications they need and the actual capabilities they possess. Although there are still no universal requirements for qualifications in the whole country, itinerant teachers are generally the teachers holding special educational qualification certificates. For example, itinerant teachers in Shanghai are required to hold corresponding teacher certificates and also Shanghai special education position certificates and to have 5 years working experience in special education with certain capabilities of organization, guidance, research, and management (Zhang, Wang, 2017, p. 4).

4.2.9. Barriers to the development of inclusive education

With around 30 years' development, the implementation of LRC has accomplished great success in increasing nationwide school enrolment of children with disabilities and making public education more accessible for them. However, the quality of LRC has been doubted by many researchers in consideration of the practical situation of many students with disabilities who have been just "sitting" instead of "learning" in regular classrooms because of several barriers to the implementation of inclusive education in China (Deng, Zhu, 2007; Deng, Zhu, 2016).

Exam-oriented value of education in China

Even though LRC has been widely recognized as the local way of implementing inclusive education in China, the cultural context of inclusive education in Western countries is quite different from that of LRC in China, where the Confucian ideology has served as the social foundation for centuries (Deng, Su, 2012, p. 85). According to the Confucian philosophy, the society is in a hierarchic structure and social members should show the behaviour corresponding to their social status. In such a social context, education has long been taken as the most popular way for upgrading the social status through the selecting system of imperial examination, which was designed for selecting the best officials for the governing group by the imperial central authority and has survived from centuries to form a highly competitive educational tradition of elitism in China (Deng, Zhu, 2016, p. 996). Based on this strong tradition, for a long time – the education in general schools has been exam-oriented and highly competitive with overemphasis on students' academic competences. As a result, all the people directly related to general school education including students, teachers, school administrators and also parents have to cope with this high pressure, which in turn affects their acceptance of LRC or inclusive education.

On the basis of the historical reason, wide acceptance and equal treatment of people with disability has not been formed in the Chinese context. People with disabilities are often regarded as disadvantaged, needing care more than education. This kind of thinking has been hold by many people and can be even found in government policies in China, which means the core values of inclusion such as equitable and appropriate education for all has not been widely accepted in the Chinese social context (Deng, Zhu, 2016, p. 996).

Moreover, as there is a huge population in China, large class sizes are another unfavourable factor in the practice of inclusive education. According to government regulations, the number of students in primary school classroom should be no more than 45 in rural areas and 50 in urban areas and the number in secondary school should be no more than 50. Yet, the real situation in many schools is that they have classes with more than 50 students. Because of the large class size, many teachers are worried that they have no spare time or energy to deal with the special needs of children with disabilities.

Contradictory attitudes to inclusive education

In the specific social context of China, people's attitudes towards inclusive education or LRC are complicated and even contradictory. According to the recent research, majority of teachers in general schools recognize that children with disabilities have equal rights to education as students without disabilities, but they still generally hold negative attitude to accepting disabled students to general classrooms and are more in favour of placing them in special schools (Zhao et al., 2016; Zhang, 2016; Zhao, Huang, 2017). Their major concerns about the difficulties of inclusive education are that students with disabilities are likely to have problems with catching up the academic performance of their classmates without disabilities and that teachers themselves lack professional knowledge of teaching disabled students (Li, 2016; Zhang, 2016; Zhao, Huang, 2017). As a result, the needs of disabled students in mainstream classrooms have often been neglected intentionally because teachers are afraid that they may disturb other students and take up teachers' time (Deng, Poon-McBrayer, 2013).

Similar attitudes to inclusive education or LRC are also held by many parents of children without disabilities in general schools and even by school administrators. Their main concerns are the potential negative effects on teaching management, academic performance of general students and unexpected circumstances threatening children's safety. In addition, it also has been found that the past experience of contacting individuals with disabilities and the understanding of inclusive education are two important influential factors of people's attitudes to LRC or to inclusive education (Zhang, Gao, 2014; Zhao, Huang, 2017).

Moreover, people's attitude to inclusive education varies according to the type of disability. To be specific, teachers are more willing to accept disabled students who are likely to be disciplined safely and conveniently, but unwilling to accept students with brain, emotional or behaviour disorders (Ma, Tan, 2010). The research shows that general teachers tend to hold the most positive attitudes to accepting children with physical disability, intellectual disability or learning disability to their classroom, but the most negative attitudes to accepting children with autism spectrum disorder or behaviour and emotional disorders in consideration of the potential difficulties of teaching management.

Imperfect policy and regulations from government

LRC is an educational policy adopted by the Chinese government to solve the problem of school enrolment for children with disabilities. By overviewing the development of LRC in China for the past 30 years, it has been found that the accomplishment of LRC has been based on the top-down administrative model that relies on government policies. Yet, until now, there has been only one specialized policy concerning LRC from the Chinese government which was issued in 1994, almost 25 years ago. As the guiding policy which came into being at the beginning of the experiment phase of LRC – when it was not mature enough, those trial measures of implementing LRC were bound to have the features of exploration and experimentation (Li, 2015, p. 17).

In the initial period, this policy played an important guiding role in the standardization and development of LRC and it became the basis for all regions in the process of formulating their local implementation methods (Li, 2015, p. 17). After about 30 years of development, no matter its scale or social background, LRC has changed dramatically. At present, it has become the mainstream way of placing children with disabilities and providing access to compulsory education for the majority of them. However, the modification of LRC policies from the government still do not meet the real needs in the practice.

On the one hand, there are no comprehensive policies and regulations at high level about LRC from the central government. In practice, the implementation of LRC depends on various regulations from the local government in different provinces and cities, which in return brings about obvious regional gaps among the whole country. On the other hand, even though LRC has been mentioned in many policies or regulations from the government, there is still lack of detailed contents pertaining to many important components of the implementation of LRC in terms of financial mechanism, teachers' qualification, workload identification of related personnel, management of inclusive school, quality supervision and evaluation, etc. The lack of sufficient details and operability of LRC policies will inevitably result in a series of problems in the process of policy implementation. One research found out that only around 30 % participants thought that the current situation of policy development and implementation was good (Wang, Yang, Zhang, 2006, p. 4).

Lack of funding guarantee

Lack of funding guarantee is another barrier to the promotion of LRC. As mentioned before, the governmental financial input to special education has dramatically increased in the last 20 years. However, the funding for LRC has been increasing slowly. Except for some local governments' conventional expenses for the work of LRC, most areas do not have a regular funding system for LRC (Peng, 2011).

A statewide study found out that there were shortages of funding for LRC in the west, middle and also east part of China. 16.5 % of the investigated general schools were without specialized funding for LRC from the local government and 38.46 % of investigated schools got only small amount of specialized funding, but only occasionally (Wang, Yang, Zhang, 2006, p. 5). For most areas and schools, the funding is far from sufficient, especially in the areas with better economic conditions with more advanced development of LRC. Insufficient funds have affected many aspects of the implementation of LRC, including teacher training, teachers' allowance, building and management of resource rooms, arrangement of teaching aids, rehabilitation equipment, and so on. Lack of funding has come to be one of the main problems of in-depth development of inclusive education in China.

Shortage of qualified LRC teachers

The quality of teachers has been attributed great importance for the development of students. The quality of inclusive teachers as well has been recognized as one of the critical factors for the promotion of inclusive education. Yet, as mentioned before, there are still no clear requirements for inclusive teachers' qualifications and corresponding certificates in the whole country, especially for the majority of inclusive teachers who directly work with disabled students in general classrooms. The poor qualifications of LRC teachers have become a serious problem for further development of LRC in China.

Discussing the situation in China, it is important to note that most of LRC teachers have graduated from colleges and universities after studying majors related to the teaching profession with teaching certificates of different subjects recognized by the government. This builds the foundation for the teaching of disabled students in general classrooms. Still, various differences among children with diverse disabilities and from children without disabilities require LRC teachers to master their basic knowledge and skills of special education.

Unfortunately, some related studies show that only 37 % of general teachers who work with disabled students have received targeted training in special education. Previous trainings have been more focused on IEP, theories of special education and inclusive education mainly in the form of theoretical lectures (Ma, Tan, 2010). In general, LRC teachers do not fully understand the educational requirements and learning characteristics of disabled students educated in regular classes and feel it is difficult to teach or guide them (Qian, Jiang, 2004). However, they have a strong desire to participate on related training programmes to improve their teaching abilities.

Generally speaking, there are many barriers to the further development of LRC in China, ranging from governmental policies to teachers' qualifications, and from abstract value of education to practical lack of funding. Among these barriers, lack of sufficient funding, teachers' insufficient knowledge and skills of special education, and an imperfect policy of preferential treatment for teachers are regarded as the three biggest problems of LRC in China (Wang, Yang, Zhang, 2006).

4.2.10. Developmental prospects of inclusive education

Along with the development of special education in China, the focus in LRC has also changed from the initial aim of increasing the admission rate of children with disabilities to improving the quality of education and from the pursuit of educational fairness at the start point to the final results.

In 2017, seven departments of the Chinese government issued the Second Special Education Promotion Plan (2017–2020). According to this plan, the school enrolment rate of children with disabilities will have reached 95 % by 2020 and the quality of LRC in general schools will improve overall. This means that LRC will continue to be a local form of inclusive education in China in the future, but the focus on implementation of LRC is improving its educational quality by the continuously increasing school enrolment rate of children with disabilities. The realization of this goal depends on the construction of a comprehensive supporting system for LRC, which covers a change of concept, improvement of the policies and mechanisms, a funding guarantee, improvement of teachers' qualifications, support from special schools and special education resource centres.

From the perspective of its origin, LRC is an educational developmental policy adopted by the Chinese government to solve the problem of school enrolment to compulsory education for a number of children with disabilities. It is a pragmatic choice for developing inclusive education under the conditions of an insufficient economic and cultural background in the biggest developing country. However, along with the development of LRC in China, this pragmatic model of inclusive education is tending to shrink and needs to pursue connotative development which aims at improving its quality (Yu, Zeng, 2017).

In order to fulfil this aim, the first step is to expand the connotation of LRC based on the core spirit of inclusive education. To be specific, the core values of LRC should be expanded from the guarantee of educational rights of children with disabilities to the equality of all individuals and respect of diversity and individual differences among all students. Therefore, the outcome of LRC should not be only the placement of disabled children in regular classrooms often called "sitting together," but the interactive way of placing children with a variety of individual differences in the same classroom called "learning together and developing together."

As the development of LRC in China has taken the top-down model, the formulation and implementation of government policies have become the strongest guarantee of LRC's development, which directly manifests the focus of the government (Wang, Yang, Zhang, 2006). Considering the lack of specialized policies concerning LRC and insufficient details of its practical mechanism, specialized policies on LRC and its detailed corresponding implementation measures are necessary to be issued by the central government as soon as possible. Among these implementation measures, funding allocation and its use, requirements from inclusive school and LRC teachers, issues of teachers' treatment, management mechanisms, mechanisms of collaboration between general school, special school and resource centre, the effective monitoring and evaluation system are the most important components to ensure high quality of LRC.

Apart from renewing the core value of LRC and the guarantee of policies and their implementation mechanisms, highly qualified teachers are another vital factor for the improving of LRC in the future. To ensure the quality of LRC teachers, clear requirements of LRC teachers' qualifications should be formulated by related departments or professional institutions, which will be taken as the criteria for selecting and hiring teachers for inclusive education.

In practice, on the one hand, all LRC in-service teachers are required to participate in training programmes of special education and pass the adequate assessment. On the other hand, the knowledge and skills concerning inclusive education and children with disabilities should be introduced to the curriculum system of colleges and universities which aim at cultivating pre-service general teachers (Peng, 2011).

Conclusion

As a local way of implementing inclusive education, LRC has been affected by the western concepts of "integration" and "mainstreaming" and is based on the core spirit of inclusive education, which respects individual's differences and aims at ensuring equal rights to education for children with disabilities. However, as a pragmatic form of inclusive education, the practice of LRC in China is not inclusive enough considering its limitation to participants and its unsatisfactory quality. However, it has been a natural choice in the particular social background of China and it has accomplished remarkable results in increasing the admission of children with disabilities.

References

Alur, M., Timmons, V. (Eds.) (2009). Inclusive education across cultures: Crossing boundaries, sharing ideas. New Delhi: SAGE Publications India Pvt Ltd.

Deng M. (2009). Inclusive education and learning in regular classrooms: Between ideals and reality. Wuhan: Huazhong Normal University Press.

Deng M., Harris K. (2008). Meeting the needs of students with disabilities in general education classrooms in China. *Journal of Teacher Education Division of the Council for Exceptional Children.* 31(3), 195–207.

Deng M., Manset, G. (2000). Analysis of the "learning in regular classrooms" movement in China. *Mental Retardation,* 38(2), 124–30.

Deng M., Poon-Macbrayer K. F., Farnsworth E. B. (2001). The development of special education in China, a sociocultural review. *Remedial and Special Education,* 22, 288–298.

Deng M., Poon-McBrayer K. F. (2013). Inclusive education in China: Conceptualization and realization. *Asia Pacific Journal of Education,* 24(2), 143–156.

Deng M., Su H. (2012). "Grafting" and "Regeneration" of integrated education in China: a social-cultural analysis. *Journal of Educational Studies,* 8 (1), 83–89.

Deng M., Xiao F. (2009). Segregation and convergence: Changes in special education paradigm. *Journal of Central China Normal University (Humanities and Social Science Edition),* 4, 134–140.

Deng M., Zhu Z.Z. (2007). The Chinese "Learning in Regular Class" and Western inclusive education: comparison and exploration. *Chinese Education and Society,* 40(4), 21–33.

Deng M., Zhu X.H. (2016). Special education reform towards inclusive education: Blurring or expanding boundaries of special and regular education in China. *Journal of Research in Special Educational Needs,* 16 (s1), 994–998.

Deng M., Zhu Zh. Y. (2007). Learning in regular classroom and inclusive education: Comparison of special education models in China and western countries. *Journal of Central China Normal University (Humanities and Social Science Edition)*, 46 (4), 125.

Department of Education and Science of UK, (1978), Special educational needs report of the committee of enquiry into the education of handicapped children and young people. http://webarchive. nationalarchives.gov.uk/20101007182820/http://sen.ttrb.ac.uk/ attachments/21739b8e-5245-4709-b433-c14b08365634.pdf (Access: March 20, 2018).

Feng Y. J. (2014). On the core professionalism of teachers in inclusive classrooms. *Chinese Journal of Special Education*, 1, 4–9.

Forlin C., Chambers D. (2011). Teacher preparation for inclusive education: increasing knowledge but raising concerns. *Asia-Pacific Journal of Teacher Education*, 39 (1), 17–32.

Gan Zh. L. (2012). From segregation to inclusion: Theory and practice of special education development. Xiamen: Xiamen University Press.

Gu D. Q. (2001). Introduction to special education. Dalian: Liaoning Normal University.

Huang P. S. (2015). A brief history of special education in China. Chengdu: Southwest Jiaotong University.

Huang Zh. Ch. (2003). Outlook of inclusive education: Thoughts on the development of inclusive education in recent 10 years. Outlook of Global Education, 5.

Hou J. J. (2001). On the influence of the evolution of human nature to special education. *Modern Special Education*, 4, 14–15.

Lei J. H. (2011). Introduction to inclusive education. Beijing: Beijing University Press.

Lei J. H., Yao H.L. (2005). Research on teachers' certification system of inclusive education. *Chinese Journal of Special Education*, 7, 43–46.

Li L. (2015). The three-decade-long developments of China's policy of inclusive education: the process, dilemma and strategies. *Chinese Journal of Special Education*, 10, 16–20.

Li X. (2016). A study of regular primary school teachers' attitude toward special students learning in regular classes. *Journal of Suihua University*, 36 (4), 20–25.

Li Y. Sh., Cai J. (2003). Inclusive education: The integration of children with disabilities into general school. *Modern Special Education*, 5, 8–9.

Li Z. H. (2013). High quality education for children with special needs. Nanjing: Nanjing Normal University Press.

Liu Sh. S., (2007). Introduction to Inclusive Education. Wuhan: Huazhong Normal University Press 4.

Ma H. Y., Tan H. P. (2010). A survey of the status quo of Shanghai teachers for special students learning in regular classes. *Chinese Journal of Special Education*, 1, 60–63, 82.

Malinen O. P. (2013). Inclusive education in China. CEREC working paper series. http://www.uta.fi/cerec/publications/workpaper/ CEREC%20Working%20Paper%204.pdf (Access: May 20, 2018).

Meng W. J. (2008). Study of teacher professional quality and standards under the view of inclusive education. *Chinese Journal of Special Education*, 5, 13–17.

Ministry of Education, (1994). Trial measures of implementing learning in regular classrooms for children and adolescents with disabilities. In: Xing T. Y., (2015). Learning in regular classroom for children with special needs. Beijing: China Light Industry Press.

Ministry of Education of People's Republic of China, (2017). Guójiā jiàoyù fāzhǎn gōngbào [National Education Development Bulletin in 2016]. http://www.moe.gov.cn/jyb_sjzl/sjzl_fztjgb/201707/ t20170710_309042.html (Access: March 20, 2018).

Ministry of Education of People's Republic of China, (2017). 2016 Nián jiàoyù tǒngjì shùjù [Education Statistics of 2016]. http:// www.moe.gov.cn/s78/A03/moe_560/jytjsj_2016/2016_qg/201708/ t20170823_311710.html (Access: March 20, 2018).

Ministry of Education of the People's Republic of China. (2017). 2016 jiaoyu fazhan tongji gongbao [National Education Development Statistical Communique of 2016]. http://www.moe.edu.cn/jyb_sjzl/ sjzl_fztjgb/201707/t20170710_309042.html,2017-07-10 (Access: May 20, 2018).

Mu Y. X. (2006). Evolution and enlightenment of special education in China. *Chinese Journal of Special Education*, 2006 (5), 37–41.

National Statistics Bureau of PRC. Statistics Communique on National Economic and Social Development of PRC in 2017. http://www.stats.

gov.cn/tjsj/zxfb/201702/t20170228_1467424.html (Access: February 28, 2017).

Peng X. G. (2011). On the challenges facing China in the promotion of inclusive education and relevant suggestions. *Chinese Journal of Special Education,* 11, 15–20.

Piao Y. X. (1995). Special education. Fuzhou: Fujian Education Press.

Piao Y. X. (1998). Efforts to develop special education disciplines with Chinese characteristics. *Special Education Research,* 1, 1–3.

Qian L. X, Jiang X. Y. (2004). An investigation report on current situation of the development of mainstreaming in China. *Chinese Journal of Special Education,* 5, 1–5.

Sanrattana U. (2010). An implementation of inclusive education. *International Journal of Education,* 33 (2), 80–85.

Save the Children (2012). A study report on the development of special education and learning in regular classroom in mainland China. Retrieved September 19, 2020, from http://www.savethechildren.org.cn/images/stories/Recource_Center/publication/report_on_learning_in_regular-class.pdf.

Sun H. L., Ding Zh. T. (2014). Empirical study on the fairness of fund input for special education based on Geordie Coefficient. *Journal of Changchun University,* 24 (1), 134–138.

Sheng Y. J. (2011). Foundation of special education. Beijing: Education Science Press.

Tian Zh. L. et al. (2015). Special education finance with educational concept of inclusion: History and present and future. *Education Research Monthly,* 1, 35–49.

United Nations Children's Fund, (2000). Defining Quality in Education. Retrieved September 19, 2020, from https://www.right-to-education.org/sites/right-to-education.org/files/resource-attachments/UNICEF_Defining_Quality_Education_2000.PDF.

UNESCO, (2009). Policy guidelines on inclusion in education. Paris, France: UNESCO.

Vaillant D. (2011). Preparing teachers for inclusive education in Latin America. Prospects. *Quarterly Review of Comparative Education,* 41 (3), 385–398.

Wang H. P. (2005). Responsibilities and evaluation of the resource room teacher at the schools with learning in regular classroom. *Chinese Journal of Special Education*, 7, 37–41.

Wang M. P., Hu P. F. (2008). Teacher's quality under the concept of inclusive education and its cultivation. *Contemporary Education Forum*, 9, 88–90.

Wang H. P., Xiao H. L. (2017). Reflections on inclusive education: related resource room teachers' work and their professional training. *Chinese Journal of Special Education*, 6, 33–36.

Wang Zh.,Yang X. J., Zhang Ch. (2006). A survey on the factors influencing quality of learning in regular classroom. *Chinese Journal of Special Education*, 5, 3–13.

Xiao F. (2005). Mainstreaming in China: history, actuality, perspectives. *Chinese Journal of Special Education*, 3, 3–6.

Xie J. R. et al. (2009). The input and use of special educational funds in the world and the implication to the development of Chinese special education. *Journal of Special Education*, 6, 17–24.

Xing T. Y. (2015). Learning in regular classroom for children with special needs. Beijing: China Light Industry Press.

Yu S. H. (2011). An investigation into the current integrated education in ordinary schools in Shanghai. *Chinese Journal of Special Education*, 4, 3–9.

Yu S. M., Zeng G. (2017). From deconstruction to reconstruction: An analysis of postmodern inclusive education. *Chinese Journal of Special Education*, 2, 3–6.

Zhang F. J, Ma H. Y., Du X. X. (2000). The history of special education in China. Shanghai: East China Normal University Press.

Zhang Y. H., Gao Y. X. (2014). An Investigation into the acceptance of inclusive education by teachers and students in regular schools and the students' parents in Xinjiang. *Chinese Journal of Special Education*, 8, 4–20.

Zhang Y. X., Wang M. M. (2017). Advances in and suggestions on the research into itinerant teachers for special-needs children learning in regular classes. *Chinese Journal of Special Education*, 1, 3–7.

Zhang Y. X. (2016). A study of regular school teachers' attitudes towards inclusive education of children with disabilities. *Journal of Educational Studies,* 12 (3), 104–113.

Zhao B. et al. (2016). Review on the related research of general education teachers' attitude towards Learning in Regular Classroom. *Journal of Suihua University,* 36 (7), 13–16.

Zhao J., Huang Sh. (2017). An investigation on the attitudes of pupils' parents towards disabled children studying in regular class in Longnan area of Gansu. *Journal of Lanzhou University of Arts and Science,* 33 (5), 4–449.

Zhao X. H., Meng W. J. (2008). Development and policy recommendations of special education during the past 30 years of China's Reform and Opening-up. *Chinese Journal of Special Education,* 10, 35–41.

Zhu N., Wang Y. (2011). Function change of special education schools in the context of inclusive education. *Chinese Journal of Special Education,* 12, 3–8.

Name Index

A

Aguiar, C. 87
Almqvist, L. 89
Alur, M. 156
Apanel, D. 15, 21
Atkinson 123

B

Bąbka, J. 21
Bailey, D. B. 90
Bal, A. 80
Balcerek, M. 14, 15
Bank-Mikkelsen, N. E. 97
Barrow, R. 99
Barry, B. 78
Bartnikowska, U. 39
Bauwens, J. 74
Bełza, M. 19
Bennett, T. 83
Bera, R. 29
Bereded-Samuel, E. 77
Berliner, D. C. 87
Bjarnason, D. J. 101
Błeszyńska, K. 39
Boettcher, C. 78
Bogucka, J. 24
Bricker, D. 90
Brown, L. 77
Bruder, M. B. 68
Brue, A. W. 99
Burke, K. 132
Burns, M. K. 83
Bush, G. W. 69
Buysse, V. 68, 90

C

Cai, J. 157
Cameto, R. 83

Carlberg, C. 73
Carta, J. J. 75
Carter, S. L. 88
Casey, A. M. 89
Chalfant, J. C. 74
Chambers, D. 182
Chirkov V. 69
Chodkowska, M. 28
Chrzanowska, I. 29
Cloninger, C. 77
Clough, P. 78
Corbett, J. 78
Crandall, J. A. 69
Ćwirynkało, K. 28
Cytowska, B. 17
Czerepaniak-Walczak, M. 26

D

Datesman, M. K. 69
De Vaus, D. A. 138
Deci, E. L. 69
Delquadri, J. 75
Deng, M. 153, 154, 156, 158, 162, 163, 166, 167, 169, 186, 187
Dennis, R. 77
Deno, E. 72, 76
Deno, S. L. 75
Doroszewska, J. 14
Du, X. X. 149, 150, 151
Dudzikowa, M. 40
Duhaney, L. 73
Dumnicka, K. 37
Dunn, L. M. 71
Dziedzic, S. 15

E

Earle, C. 132

Edelman, S. 77
Edgar, G. 76
Epanchin, B. C. 74, 75

F
Fairbairn, G. 24
Fairbairn, S. 24
Farnsworth, E. B. 163
Feng, Y. J. 183
Firkowska-Mankiewicz,
  A. 19, 22
Fletcher, J. M. 83
Forlin, C. 98, 132, 133, 134,
  138, 182
Forness, S. R. 79
Franiok, P. 14, 15, 17
Friedman, M. 75
Friend, M. 74, 75
Fuchs, D. 73, 79
Fuchs, L. S. 73, 79
Furedi, F. 52

G
Gagné 69 see Deci
Gajdzica, Z. 14, 15, 17, 19, 21,
  23, 25, 29, 32, 36, 39, 41, 42,
  48, 49, 54
Gan, Zh. L. 152
Gao, Y. X. 188
Garbat, M. 23
Giami, A. 124
Giangreco, M. F. 77
Gidley, J. 77, 78
Greenwood, C. R. 75
Gresham, F. M. 79
Griffin, K. W. 78
Grzyb, B. 35
Gu, D. Q. 152
Guralnick 68 see Bruder
Gustavsson, A. 24
Guzik-Tkacz, M. 19

H
Haager, D. 75
Hájková, V. 100
Hall, R. V. 75
Hallahan, D. P. 79
Hampson, G. 77
Harris, K. 169
Hartl, P. 123
Hinz, A. 18
Hou, J. J. 164
Hourcade, J. J. 74
Hu, P. F. 183
Huang, P. S. 150
Huang, Sh. 187, 188
Huang, Zh. Ch. 156
Hulek, A. 15
Hull, K. 99

I
Idol, L. 74

J
Jachimczak, B. 29
Javitz, H. 83
Jesenský, J. 98, 102
Jian, Z. 152
Jiang, X. Y. 190
Jimerson, S. R. 83

K
Kaplan 69 see Chirkov
Kauffman, J. M. 73, 79
Kavale, K. 73
Kazanowski, Z. 28, 29, 39
Kearny, E. N. 69
Kelleher, C. 89
Kim 69 see Chirkov
Kirenko, J. 28
Klus-Stańska, D. 47
Kochanowska, E. 43
Kochhar-Bryant, C. A. 76

Kocurová, M. 99
Korczyński, M. 29
Kościelska, M. 24
Koselleck, R. 22, 23
Kowalik, S. 51
Krause, A. 22, 23, 24
Kruk-Lasocka, J. 19
Kupisiewicz, Cz. 19
Kupisiewicz, M. 19
Kwiatkowska, H. 40

L
Lee, S. W. 89
Lei, J. H. 157, 160, 161, 183
Lewis, R. B. 88
Lewowicki, T. 18
Li, L. 188
Li, X. 187
Li, Y. Sh. 157
Li, Z. H. 176, 177
Ligus, R. 19
Liu, Sh. S. 157, 159
Loreman, T. 132
Loveland, T. 74
Loxley, A. 18, 45

M
Ma, H. Y. 149, 150, 151, 184,
   188, 190
Macek, P. 124
MacMillan, D. L. 79
Malinen, O. P. 162
Manset, G. 163
Mareš, J. 39
Mastropieri, M. A. 73, 74,
   132
McLeskey, J. 71, 72, 74
McWilliam, R. A. 67, 72, 86,
   87, 89, 90
Męczkowska, A. 40
Meng, W. J. 152, 153, 154,
   183

Milerski, B. 19
Minczakiewicz, E. 43
Mu, Y. X. 150, 151, 152, 154
Murch, T. 75
Murray, W. 151

N
Nevin, A. 74
Newman, L. 83
Niileksela, C. R. 89
Nikitorowicz, J. 28

O
Odom, S. L. 68, 81
Ogrodzka-Mazur, E. 18
Okoń, W. 19, 44, 45
Olszewski, S. 19
Ostrowska, A. 28

P
Paolucci-Whitcomb, P. 74
Parys, K. 19
Peng, X. G. 189, 192
Piao, Y. X. 155, 162
Pielecki, A. 28, 29, 39
Półturzycki, J. 45
Poon-Mcbrayer, K. F. 163, 166, 187
Potměšil, M. 101
Power, T. J. 89
Průcha, J. 39, 98

Q
Qi, P. Y. 180
Qian, L. X. 190

R
Rafferty, Y. 78
Reagan, R. 69
Reynolds, M. C. 72
Rieser, R. 24
Riley-Tillman, T. C. 89
Roosevelt, T. 69

Rosenshine, B. V. 87
Ryan 69 see Chirkov

S
Salend, S. 73
Sanrattana, U. 182
Schattman, R. 77
Schumm, J. S. 75
Scruggs, T. E. 73, 74, 132
Sękowski, A. 28
Shade, R. A. 132
Shakespeare, T. 123
Sharma, U. 132
Sheng, Y. J. 162
Siegień-Matyjewicz, A. 19
Sims, J. 89
Skibska, J. 29
Śliwerski, B. 19
So, T.-s. H. 74
Soukakou, E. 68
Sovák, M. 101, 102
Speck, O. 24
Stainback, S. 72
Stainback, W. 72
Stewart, R. 131
Su, H. 162, 186
Sullivan, A. L. 80
Sutherland, C. 132
Swanson, K. 74
Szabała, B. 28
Szczurek-Boruta, A. 18
Szewczuk, W. 44
Szkudlarek, T. 18
Szumski, G. 18, 19, 21, 24

T
Tan, H. P. 184, 188, 190
Thomas, G. 18, 45
Tian, Zh. L. 178, 179, 180,
   181, 182
Timmons, V. 156
Tuohy, D. 39

V
Vaillant, D. 182
Valdes, K. 83
Van Dusen Pysh, M. 74
VanDerHeyden, A. M. 83
Vaughn, S. 75, 83
Vávra, M. 123

W
Wagner, M. 83
Walberg, H. J. 72
Waldron, N. 74
Walterovà, E. 39
Wang, H. P. 184, 185
Wang, M. C. 72
Wang, M. P. 183
Wang, Y. 170
Wang, Zh. 180, 189,
   190, 192
Waszkiewicz, A. 37
Watson, N. 124
Wawer, R. 28
Wei, Y. X. 180
Wesley, P. W. 90
Wheeler, L. 77, 88
Whorton, D. 75
Wilcox, M. J. 75
Will, M. 72
Wilmshurst, L. 99
Winthrop, J. 70
Wójcik, M. 39
Wolfensberger, W. 76, 90
Woods, J. J. 75
Woods, R. 99
Wyczesany, J. 14, 15

X
Xianji, L. 152
Xiao, F. 156, 163
Xiao, H. L. 184
Xie, J. R. 179, 180, 182
Xing, T. Y. 171, 172

Y
Yang, X. J. 180, 189, 190, 192
Yao, H. L. 183
Yisheng, L. 157
Yu, S. H. 178
Yu, S. M. 191
Yuexian, Z. 152

Z
Zacharuk, T. 24
Zakrzewska-Manterys, E. 24
Zamkowska, A. 19, 21, 43
Zeng, G. 191

Zhang, C. 83
Zhang, Ch. 180, 189, 190, 192
Zhang, F. J. 149, 150, 151
Zhang, Y. H. 188
Zhang, Y. X. 185, 187
Zhao, B. 180, 187
Zhao, J. 187, 188
Zhao, X. H. 152, 153, 154
Zhu, N. 170
Zhu, X. H. 167, 186, 187
Zhu, Zh. Y. 158, 162, 186
Zieliński, J. 28

Studies in Social Sciences, Philosophy and History of Ideas

Edited by Andrzej Rychard

Vol. 1   Józef Niżnik: Twentieth Century Wars in European Memory. 2013.

Vol. 2   Szymon Wróbel: Deferring the Self. 2013.

Vol. 3   Cain Elliott: Fire Backstage. Philip Rieff and the Monastery of Culture. 2013.

Vol. 4   Seweryn Blandzi: Platon und das Problem der Letztbegründung der Metaphysik. Eine historische Einführung. 2014.

Vol. 5   Maria Gołębiewska / Andrzej Leder/Paul Zawadzki (éds.): L'homme démocratique. Perspectives de recherche. 2014.

Vol. 6   Zeynep Talay-Turner: Philosophy, Literature, and the Dissolution of the Subject. Nietzsche, Musil, Atay. 2014.

Vol. 7   Saidbek Goziev: Mahalla – Traditional Institution in Tajikistan and Civil Society in the West. 2015.

Vol. 8   Andrzej Rychard / Gabriel Motzkin (eds.): The Legacy of Polish Solidarity. Social Activism, Regime Collapse, and the Building of a New Society. 2015.

Vol. 9   Wojciech Klimczyk / Agata Świerzowska (eds.): Music and Genocide. 2015.

Vol. 10   Paweł B. Sztabiński / Henryk Domański / Franciszek Sztabiński (eds.): Hopes and Anxieties in Europe. Six Waves of the European Social Survey. 2015.

Vol. 11   Gavin Rae: Privatising Capital. The Commodification of Poland´s Welfare State. 2015.

Vol. 12   Adriana Mica / Jan Winczorek / Rafał Wiśniewski (eds.): Sociologies of Formality and Informality. 2015.

Vol. 13   Henryk Domański: The Polish Middle Class. Translated by Patrycja Poniatowska. 2015.

Vol. 14   Henryk Domański: Prestige. Translated by Patrycja Poniatowska. 2015.

Vol. 15   Cezary Wodziński: Heidegger and the Problem of Evil. Translated into English by Agata Bielik-Robson and Patrick Trompiz. 2016.

Vol. 16   Maria Gołębiewska (ed.): Cultural Normativity. Between Philosophical Apriority and Social Practices. 2017.

Vol. 17   Anita Williams: Psychology and Formalisation. Phenomenology, Ethnomethodology and Statistics. 2017.

Vol. 18   Mikołaj Pawlak: Tying Micro and Macro. 2018.

Vol. 19   Franciszek Sztabiński / Henryk Domański / Paweł B. Sztabiński (eds.): New Uncertainties and Anxieties in Europe. Seven Waves of the European Social Survey. 2018.

Vol. 20   Adriana Mica / Katarzyna M. Wyrzykowska / Rafał Wiśniewski / Iwona Zielińska (eds.): Sociology of the Invisible Hand. 2018.

Studies in Philosophy, Culture and Contemporary Society

Edited by Bogusław Paź

Vol. 21   Jan Felicjan Terelak: Psychology of the Operator of Technical Devices. 2019.

Vol. 22   Dorota Maria Leszczyna: Del idealismo al realismo crítico. La política como realización en José Ortega y Gasset. 2019.

Vol. 23   Zbigniew Drozdowicz: La république des savants. Sans révérence. Traduit du polonais par Catherine Popczyk. 2019.

Vol. 24   Andrzej Waśkiewicz: The Idea of Political Representation and Its Paradoxes. Translated from Polish by Agnieszka Waśkiewicz and Marilyn Burton. 2019.

Vol. 25   Ilona Błocian / Dmitry Prokudin (eds.): Imagination – Art, Science and Social World. 2019.

Vol. 26   Zbigniew Drozdowicz: Faces of the Enlightenment. Philosophical sketches. 2019.

Vol. 27   Włodzimierz Piątkowski: From Medicine to Sociology. Health and Illness in Magdalena Sokołowska's Research Conceptions. 2020.

Vol. 28   Roman Witold Ingarden: Die Mitschriften von den Vorlesungen Martin Heideggers über die Phänomenologische Interpretation von Kants *Kritik der reinen Vernunft* (Wintersemester 1927/28). Aus dem Manuskript abgeschrieben und das Vorwort verfasst haben: Radosław Kuliniak und Mariusz Pandura. 2020.

Vol. 29   Krzysztof Wielecki / Klaudia Śledzińska (eds.): The Relational Theory of Society. Archerian Studies vol. 2. 2020.

Vol. 30   Zenon Gajdzica / Robin McWilliam / Miloň Potměšil / Guo Ling: Inclusive Education of Learners with Disability – The Theory versus Reality . 2020.

www.peterlang.com